Rowing Tales

Rowperfect UK

Rowing Tales

Copyright 2017 by Rowperfect UK

All rights reserved. No part of this publication may be reproduced or transmitted in any form by any means, electronic or mechanical, including photocopy, or any information storage or retrieval system, without written permission of the publisher, except in cases of brief quotation by reviewers or commentators. Printed in the U.K.

First Printing: October 2017

Rowperfect UK
52 Broadway
Duffield
Derbyshire DE56 4BU
United Kingdom
www.rowperfect.co.uk

Dedication

This book is dedicated to every athlete, parent, coxswain and coach who has ever sat on a riverbank or stood in a bar talking rowing with their friends – and enjoyed it.

From the Publisher

Everyone has a rowing story to tell.

I first got the idea for **Rowing Tales** when I read *My Old Man*, a compilation book of stories about Fathers. It dawned on me that rowing has its own collection of anecdotes, and maybe this could become Rowperfect's newest project, an anthology about rowing.

I have my own personal collection of tales. During the past twelve months as I've interviewed and recorded and transcribed and written up the tales which have been submitted, I kept thinking about which of my own rowing tales to record.

There's the one about swapping sides as a novice, or making three French fisherman belly-laugh as I rammed the river bank in front of them, of Phil fixing up the seat racing in order to de-select me from the first boat, or the time the new kit arrived in the wrong colour, of fund raising sponsored rows, or the biggest raffle in rowing history to win a single shell and an ergo, of colourful insults (old goats), or fun times head racing in a double and gaining ground on a coxed-four under the very narrow bridge at Bedford.

Instead, I decided that this book should not be about my writing. I write weekly in the Rowperfect News blog, I broadcast monthly on the RowingChat podcast. This book needs to be the voice of everyone else - but me.

And I'm grateful – for the insights and wry smiles as the many, many contributors have given me their stories, and for the stories themselves. And also to Peter Mallory for editing and formatting the collection.

I hope you enjoy this book. Leave it by the bed, in the bathroom, in the boathouse. Let others dip in and read, or send a copy to an old rowing friend.

And if it inspires you to tell me your rowing tale – by all means send it by email to *becky@rowperfect.co.uk*. When we get enough, we'll do a second volume. It could become an annual publication.

Above all, keep rowing, keep coaching, keep coxing, keep recruiting and keep supporting this wonderful sport of ours.

Rebecca Caroe, Publisher
Auckland, New Zealand
1 October 2017

Introduction

Most rowers I know have a favourite story, a favourite rowing tale, and each one is unique. Here is a collection of them, some old, some new, spanning the world. Enjoy.

Peter Mallory, Editor
Old Oar Cottage
Los Angeles, California
1 October 2017

Peter Mallory is the author of ***The Sport of Rowing***, published in four volumes in 2011 by The River & Rowing Museum in Henley-on-Thames, England, the author of ***An Out-of-Boat Experience, 3rd Edition***, published in eBook form in 2014 by Rowperfect UK, the editor of the 2013-14 eBook presentation of the updated ***Fairbairn on Rowing***, also published by Rowperfect UK, and co-author of ***Leander Club: the First 200 Years***, published by Leander in 2018. For more information, see *www.rowingevolution.com*.

Authors

Charles Dickens 18

Herman Melville 20

Christopher Dodd 24

Steve Fairbairn 28

George Pocock 29

Andrew O'Brien 30

Andrew Triggs Hodge 32

Steve Fairbairn 34

Adrian Ellison 37

Jeff Klepacki and Jamie Koven 39

Don Breitenberg 41

Duncan Holland 42

Boris Starling 43

Alistair Potts 47

Charles Sweeney 51

Wanaka Rowing Club 58

Peter Mallory 62

Bruce Lodder 68

Matt Langridge 72

Joe Burk 74

Tom Weil 76

Mike Davenport 82

Drew Ginn 85

Mary Boland 88

Ann Hewitt 89

Rory Gullan 90

Stuart Harrison 94

Jen Kilby 100

Kirsty Dunhill 101

Stan Pocock 103

Eric Mahoney 104

Tina Duff-Dobson 106

Tonia Williams 107

Chelsea Dommert 109

Marty Zuehlke 114

Sue and Bryan Storey 115

Dudley Storey 119

Göran Buckhorn 125

Volker Nolte 128

George Bridgewater 132

Xeno Müller 136

Frans Göbel 138

Charles Dickens

Competitive rowing has been practiced since Classical times and before. Greek heroes in Homer's *Iliad* and *Odyssey* were famous for their skills at the oar.

Beginning at least as early as the 1600s, professional rowing competitions were a common sight on the Thames in London, where they drew huge crowds. Here is a description of one such event by the English novelist Charles Dickens, published in *Bell's Life in London* on 23 August 1835.

The River – Above Bridge[1]
A Sketch by a Celebrated Artist

A well-contested rowing match on the Thames is a very lively and interesting scene. The water is studded with boats of all sorts, kinds, and descriptions — places in the coal-barges at the different wharfs are let to crowds of spectators — beer and tobacco flow freely about — men, women, and children, wait for the start in breathless expectation — cutters of six and eight oars glide gently up and down, waiting to accompany their proteges during the race — bands of music add to the animation if not to the harmony of the scene — groups of watermen are assembled at the different stairs discussing the merits of the respective candidates — and the prize wherry, which is rowed slowly about by a pair of sculls, is an object of general interest. Two o'clock

---

[1] In Dickens' time, the Thames River was separated into two sections, Above Bridge and Below Bridge, by Old London Bridge, which for many centuries had been the only bridge that crossed the river anyway near London.

strikes, and everybody looks anxiously in the direction of the bridge through which the candidates for the prize will come — half-past two, and the general attention which has been preserved so long begins to flag, when suddenly a gun is heard, and the noise of distant hurraing along each bank of the river — every head is bent forward — the noise draws nearer and nearer — the boats which have been waiting at the bridge start briskly up the river — a well manned gaffey shoots through the arch, the sitters cheering on the boats behind them, which are not yet visible — "Here they are" is the general cry — and through darts the first boat, the men in her stripped to the skin, and exerting every muscle to preserve the advantage they have gained — four other boats follow close astern, there are not two boats' length between them — the shouting is tremendous, and the interest intense. "Go on, Pink" — "Give it her, Red" — "Sulliwin for ever" — "Brayvo ! George" — "Now, Tom, now—now—vy don't your partner stretch out?" — "Two pots to a pint on yellow," &c. &c. Every little public-house fires its gun and hoists its flag; and the men who win the heat come in amidst a splashing and shouting, and banging and confusion, which no one can imagine who has not witnessed it, and of which any description would convey a very faint idea.

Herman Melville

In "The Pequod Meets the Virgin", Chapter 81 of the immortal *Moby Dick; or The Whale*, published in 1851, author Herman Melville describes a rowing race between the whaling boats of two ships, the *Pequod* out of Nantucket, Massachusetts under Captain Ahab, and the *Jungfrau* out of Bremen, in what is now Germany, under Captain Derick De Deer. The race was characterised by the most colourful exhortations from the coxswains and was decided by an unfortunate crab.

A Righteous Judgment

Whales were almost simultaneously raised from the mast-heads of both vessels, and so eager for the chase was Derick that he slewed round his boat and made after the leviathan lamp-feeders.[2]

Now, the game having risen to leeward, he and the other three German boats that soon followed him, had considerably the start of the Pequod's keels. There were eight whales... They left a great, wide wake, as though continually unrolling a great wide parchment upon the sea.

Full in this rapid wake, and many fathoms in the rear, swam a huge, humped old bull... With one intent all the combined rival boats were pointed for this one fish...

At this juncture, the Pequod's keels had shot by the three German boats last lowered, but from the great start he had had, Derick's boat still led the chase, though

---

[2] A lamp-feeders was a small cup with a spout to insert oil into a lamp. Whales were the repositories of many hundreds of gallons of sperm oil, which fed the lamps of the world during the 19th century.

every moment neared by his foreign rivals. The only thing they feared, was, that from being already so nigh to his mark, he would be enabled to dart his iron before they could completely overtake and pass him. As for Derick, he seemed quite confident that this would be the case, and occasionally with a deriding gesture shook his lamp-feeder[3] at the other boats.

"I tell ye what it is, men" – cried Stubb to his crew – "It's against my religion to get mad; but I'd like to eat that villainous Yarman[4] – Pull – won't ye? Are ye going to let that rascal beat ye? Do ye love brandy? A hogshead of brandy, then, to the best man. Come, why don't some of ye burst a blood-vessel? Who's that been dropping an anchor overboard – we don't budge an inch – we're becalmed. Halloo, here's grass growing in the boat's bottom – and by the Lord, the mast there's budding. This won't do, boys. Look at that Yarman! The short and long of it is, men, will ye spit fire or not?"

"Oh! see the suds he makes!" cried Flask, dancing up and down – "What a hump – Oh, do pile on the beef – lays like a log! Oh! my lads, do spring – slap-jacks and quohogs for supper, you know, my lads – baked clams and muffins – oh, do, do spring – he's a hundred barreler – don't lose him now – don't, oh, don't! – see that Yarman – Oh! won't ye pull for your duff, my lads – such a sog! such a sogger! Don't ye love sperm? There goes three thousand dollars, men! – a bank! – a whole bank! The bank of England! – Oh, do, do, do! – What's that Yarman about now?"

---

[3] Captain De Deer had in his hand an oil can and an actual lamp-feeder, which he had brought to the Pequod to beg for some oil. The *Jungfrau* had run out.
[4] An obviously pejorative term of unknown meaning. Melville uses it only in this chapter of *Moby Dick*.

At this moment Derick was in the act of pitching his lamp-feeder at the advancing boats, and also his oil-can; perhaps with the double view of retarding his rivals' way, and at the same time economically accelerating his own by the momentary impetus of the backward toss.

"The unmannerly Dutch dogger!" cried Stubb. "Pull now, men, like fifty thousand line-of-battle-ship loads of red-haired devils. What d'ye say, Tashtego; are you the man to snap your spine in two-and-twenty pieces for the honor of old Gay-head? What d'ye say?"

"I say, pull like god-dam," – cried the Indian.

Fiercely, but evenly incited by the taunts of the German, the Pequod's three boats now began ranging almost abreast; and, so disposed, momentarily neared him. In that fine, loose, chivalrous attitude of the headsman when drawing near to his prey, the three mates stood up proudly, occasionally backing the after oarsman with an exhilarating cry of, "There she slides, now! Hurrah for the white-ash[5] breeze! Down with the Yarman! Sail over him!"

But so decided an original start had Derick had, that spite of all their gallantry, he would have proved the victor in this race, had not a righteous judgment descended upon him in a crab which caught the blade of his midship oarsman. While this clumsy lubber was striving to free his white-ash, and while, in consequence, Derick's boat was nigh to capsizing, and he thundering away at his men in a mighty rage; – that was a good time for Starbuck, Stubb, and Flask. With a shout, they took a mortal start forwards, and slantingly ranged up on the German's quarter. An instant more, and all four boats were diagonically in the whale's immediate wake,

---

[5] Refers to oars, which were made of white ash.

while stretching from them, on both sides, was the foaming swell that he made...

Seeing now that but a very few moments more would give the Pequod's boats the advantage, and rather than be thus foiled of his game, Derick chose to hazard what to him must have seemed a most unusually long dart, ere the last chance would for ever escape.

But no sooner did his harpooneer stand up for the stroke, than all three tigers – Queequeg, Tashtego, Daggoo – instinctively sprang to their feet, and standing in a diagonal row, simultaneously pointed their barbs; and darted over the head of the German harpooneer, their three Nantucket irons entered the whale. Blinding vapors of foam and white-fire! The three boats, in the first fury of the whale's headlong rush, bumped the German's aside with such force, that both Derick and his baffled harpooneer were spilled out, and sailed over by the three flying keels.

"Don't be afraid, my butter-boxes[6]," cried Stubb, casting a passing glance upon them as he shot by; "ye'll be picked up presently – all right – I saw some sharks astern – St. Bernard's dogs, you know – relieve distressed travellers. Hurrah!"

---

[6] A pejorative British term for a Dutch person, presumably referring to the orange stripe at the top of old Dutch flags. It was common in the 19th century for non-Europeans to conflate Dutch and Deutsch.

Christopher Dodd

One need not look back to a previous century to find great prose writing about the sport of rowing. British journalist and historian Christopher Dodd has written about rowing for forty years. Prolific author, board member of the Friends of Rowing History and co-founder of the River & Rowing Museum at Henley-on-Thames, he has been rowing correspondent to *The Guardian* newspaper for decades.

It has been 125 years since delegates from Belgium, France, Netherlands, Italy and Switzerland met in Turin and launched the Fédération Internationale des Sociétés d'Aviron (FISA). To celebrate, the international federation recently invited members of the world rowing family to share some of their experiences. Here is Chris recalling the inaugural meeting of the newly-formed Media Commission in 1991, which had a surprising twist.

The Swiss Joke

In 1991 FISA's annual meeting of all the commissions took place in Zagreb. Having never been to the area, I set off a few days early to explore before rowing matters intervened. Hardly had I reached Heathrow, however, when shots were fired in an unheard of corner of Croatia, the village of Pakrac, a few hours drive east of Zagreb. What few realised at the time, including yours truly, was that the countries of fragile Yugoslavia were sliding into a Balkan war. These were the first shots.

My only knowledge of the region's history came from Olivia Manning's Balkan trilogy. But my boss at the *Guardian* newspaper was keen to have a story from a man who happened to be on the ground. That is how I became a war reporter.

I hired a car and a student interpreter from the FISA conference, and we set off to Pakrac and parked near the village square. Two Yugoslav army tanks – or were they Croatian Defence Force? – eye-balled the sand-bagged police station across the way, while Orthodox and Catholic churches faced each other from opposite sides. There were bullet holes in masonry and 'Greater Serbia' daubs on walls. The tank man chatted while enjoying a cigarette; the police wouldn't let us in; both priests declined an interview. Eventually we repaired to a café where locals told stories of rumour and atrocity that certainly qualified as fake news. On the way back to Zagreb my student took me to the terrifying museum at Jasenovac, site of an extermination camp run by the Ustaše in WW2.

Pakrac was clearly not a joke. Next day the *Guardian* was granted an interview by president Franjo Tuđman, and somehow I concocted a story that likened Croatian-Serbian relations to the Wild West. I can claim to have trod carefully while unravelling very little.

But I digress. The FISA joint commissions meeting was about to start. Its form is that commissions meet separately or in pairs for a day or two and then come together for a joint session with the executive and council.

The media's agenda involved discussions with athletes, medics, youth and women's commissions to explore increasing publicity and improving press relations, etc. But my chief concern was another *Guardian* assignment that had come my way because of my frequent visits to Switzerland on rowing business. Namely, to write about Switzerland's anniversary of 700 years as a state, and specifically, whether the Swiss had a sense of humour.

Our chairman was Paul Kölliker, a genial, very tall journalist from Lucerne (who had a short and wide colleague, thus dubbing the pair the 'gnomes of Zurich'). Who better to point the way to an answer? I interrupted his first words by saying, 'Paul, never mind about issues like how to explain the concept of repêchage to the public – the most important question is: Are the Swiss capable of enjoying a joke?'

'Kreeeeeeessss', he said – he always called me Kreeeeeeessss – 'I will tell you a true story:

'One day I was climbing Pilatus [the mountain that broods over Lucerne] when half way up I crossed the path for walkers and was surprised to see a small car with Austrian number plates reversing up the mountain. As I passed I asked the driver, 'Why are you driving in reverse?' He replied, 'In case there is no turning circle at the top!'

'I carried on and then, several hours later, when I was walking down the mountain, I met the car again, still in reverse. I asked, 'Why are you still in reverse?' Full of excitement, the driver answered, 'Because there was a turning circle at the top!'

For the next day and a half, Paul told a stream of jokes, Swiss jokes, many at the expense of Austrians, most of them unrepeatable in a family setting. Our meeting room rocked with laughter (and continued to do so for all the years that the commission sat), and Zagreb's conference centre corridor echoed with mirth.

On the last morning, the media commissioners took their seats for the plenary session. In his opening remark of his opening remarks, president Denis Oswald, a Swiss lawyer who was presiding over his first joint commissions meeting, demanded to know the cause of the commotion exuded from media sessions throughout the proceedings.

As the designated spokesperson for the commission, I rose to my feet and declared that we had made a ground-breaking discovery in cultural understanding. The FISA media commission had unmasked a sense of humour in president Oswald's countrymen, whether their native tongue is French like his or *Schwiizerdütsch* like Kölliker's.

The evidence appeared in a piece entitled 'The Swiss, 700 Fears On' in the *Guardian* on 19 July 1991.

Steve Fairbairn

Rowing has always elicited such passion from its participants that it is no surprise that occasional works of truly stirring poetry have resulted.

Our first selection comes from Australian-born Steve Fairbairn, perhaps the most influential (and controversial) individual our sport has ever produced. Coaches the world over can quote from this poem by heart.

The Oarsman's Song

The willowy sway of the hands away
And the water boiling aft,
The elastic spring and the steely fling
That drives the flying craft.
The steely spring and the musical ring
Of the blade with the biting grip,
And the stretching draw of the bending oar
That rounds the turn with a whip.
And the lazy float that runs the boat,
And makes the swing quite true,
And gives the rest that the oarsman blest
As he drives the blade right through.
All through the swing he hears the boat sing
As she guides on her flying track,
And he gathers aft to strike the craft
With a ringing bell-note crack.
From stretcher to oar with drive and draw,
He speeds the boat along.
All whalebone and steel and a willowy feel –
That is the oarsman's song.

George Pocock

Our second selection is from George Pocock, legendary 20th Century American boat builder and rowing philosopher in Seattle, Washington, prominently featured in the recent best-seller, *The Boys in the Boat*.

Pocock's family had constructed racing shells for many generations in Britain. His father had been the boat builder at Eton College, his sister was Champion of the Thames, his brother won Doggett's Coat and Badge, and only a workshop accident stood in George's way to his own Coat and Badge at the end of his own rowing apprenticeship.

Symphony of Motion

It's a great art, is rowing.
It's the finest art there is.
It's a symphony of motion.
When you're doing well,
Why it's nearing perfection.
And when you reach perfection,
You are touching the divine.
It touches the you of you,
Which is your soul.

Andrew O'Brien

Andrew O'Brien, a stalwart at Rowing Victoria in British Columbia, Canada, also has a bit of the poet in him.

One Stroke in a Row

We all have one perfect rowing stroke in us; most of us haven't taken it yet.

One day, after one more lucky dip of the oar, after we have labored through countless turgid puddles, it will come to us. It will take perfect form in a small, swirling vortex. It will slide away beyond the stern to live its brief life, a diminishing echo of our daring… a tiny shard of our toil. It will be simple: a transparent eddy slipping away to a watery horizon…

And the water… well, it will hardly notice, but we will notice.

With one stroke, we will see the evolution of splash into triumph; a heart's hammering into music. We will be that rower, that silent audience of one, absorbed by the improvisational performance of a puddle, and feel in our swelling chest its fading expansive completeness.

And if we are fortunate, that one puddle, that one ephemeral record of a perfect moment in time, will have whirling equals, duplicated in a crew's poised collaboration, each identical stroke slipping through water in confident lockstep. Spiraling footprints in formation – marching sentinels to left and right, port and starboard, their short lives dedicated to our boat's untroubled wake.

In that brief, lingering moment, when we are wishing our stroke farewell and a long life (just before we free the wheels to travel the long-slide again), we will hear beneath our hull, maybe for the first and last time, the mythical bubbles of rowing perfection.

Andrew Triggs Hodge

Poetry can be found when you least expect it. Before Andrew Triggs Hodge won three Olympic and four World Gold Medals for Great Britain, he began his rowing career at the Staffordshire University Boat Club in the English Midlands.

Rudyard Lake

It was another cold winter's start, piling into the minibus to take the crew out of Stoke-on-Trent and into the Peak District. The sun would not rise for some time yet, and the temperature was biting. I took whatever kit I had, put it all on, and we drove away from urban street lights into the clean, crisp darkness of a rural starlight morning.

We gingerly pulled the boat from its rack, a four with its bowside riggers missing. There wasn't room otherwise in that little shed. As the warmth from the bus left our fingers, we fumbled and scrapped and got the riggers on, this dire ritual of circumstance necessary to allow our uni crew to boat onto Rudyard Lake.

The darkness was solemn, observing our every move as we shuffled the boat down the steps and onto the pontoon. As we set the boat onto the water, no one noticed the first ripples to break on a lake that might not have seen a wave for generations. This was our lake, where arrogant, misguided youth pissed and spat and demanded no recourse.

We pushed away into the night, took our first strokes, Gunga Din toiling and aching. Pitch darkness surrounded us. We rowed, less cutting through the silk, more smashing holes in glass.

But even this wasn't enough to destroy what came next. Even before the nascent sun could make its first impression on the horizon, the woods all around us rising from the lake's banks started to glisten and sparkle, only a few at first, but with every minute more and more found the confidence to glint and wink. It wasn't long before our little crew was surrounded by radiance, a heavy frost reflecting each and every ray of new sunlight.

Time passed, and the lake revealed a delicate band of mist not a foot above its surface – an impossible image, perfection personified in a single sheet of immaculate glass that stretched from bank to bank. And through this band of mist we rowed, stroke by stroke, cutting a wake that arced out behind us. Not even our smashing and driving could prevent this wake from its natural course, expanding and flowing to each shore.

This image will stay with me forever. The rowing surely was part of it, but really it was the lake, the trees, and the winter combining as they sometimes do. Once in a while a lucky oarsman bears witness to nature at its most glorious.

Steve Fairbairn

There always has been poetic beauty in close rowing competition. In the reminiscence below from his memoir, *Fairbairn of Jesus*, Steve Fairbairn, who did the majority of his rowing and coaching in Cambridge and London in Great Britain, recalls the 1885 contest between the two Cambridge University Boat Club Trial Eights, important to rowing history because that was the moment he surreptitiously introduced longer slides to University rowing.

Spurts and Counter-Spurts

The closest and best race I rowed was in the Cambridge Trial Eights of 1885 [prior to the 1886 Boat Race]. At this time, I had coached nearly every college at Cambridge and knew their capabilities. I was helping the President to coach the Trials and rowed in one, as I always did.

We had in our Trial Eight my College Stroke [C.H. Bicknell] and myself 7. We had just won the Grand at Henley, and as 6 we had the Cambridge 6 of the two previous years [E.W. Haig], my brother [Tom] 5, then First Trinity men 4, 3, and 2, and a Jesus man bow. The other crew had the famous C.J. Bristowe stroke [1886 Blue Boat bow, 1887 Blue Boat stroke, both winning efforts], I think Barclay and Muttlebury 7 and 6, the following year's Cambridge 7 and 6 and the Cambridge 4 at 4, and 3, 2, and bow Trinity Hall men who won the Grand in '86 and '87. So we were two hot crews.

I went down in the train to Ely smoking a cigar, the intention being to make the other Trial think we did not mean to go for a blood race, and so hoping they would start quietly and let us get a good lead.

No. 6 and I got two screw-drivers and lengthened our slides two inches forward. It was in the best interests of rowing to show that a crew could win a long-distance race with longer slides.

We rowed for three miles from the bridge where the race now finishes to the next bridge. We had arranged to dash off at a hundred yards' pace, get a big lead, and row a waiting race in front – as trial eight-oared races so frequently were more processions than races.

Off we went at thirty-eight to the minute in heavy ships, but to my surprise the other crew led us, though we were going remarkably well. They led by more than a bow canvas at the end of a minute or so, and to stop them going away, I had to call on our crew for an effort.

Every man rowing his last ounce, we slowly crept up and forged ahead about ten feet. Then began a series of spurts and counter-spurts. The other crew forged ahead, and I called once more and we forged ahead. This seemed to go on for miles, just like a swimming race with the two competitors swimming out of time, first one and then the other forging ahead at each stroke. After what seemed a very long time I caught sight of a tall chimney which I knew was only half-way, and I knew our crew could not get as far again with continuous spurts, so I gasped out to the stroke:

"Swing out, we're only half-way."

We swung out and settled down.

The other crew drew away inch by inch and looked as if they must leave us, but when they got three-quarters of a length ahead they stuck there. Our hearts were coming round and they were killing themselves trying to get away. I had made up my mind not to let their rudder out of sight, as when that happens the breaking-point soon comes. When I felt able to do so, I called on our crew, who were more than holding them, and we closed with them, got level, drew away, and got our rudder out of sight and stayed there for the last half mile.

Both boats drew into the bank and the sixteen men got out and lay down side by side, puffing and tired, but happy. Nothing gives such supreme contentment as lying down exhausted, and healthily recovering after a struggle such as we had had. No one said a word. We lay there for ten minutes, got back into the boats, and paddled home, and then I told the President that we had lengthened the slides. That was the end of short slides, which would never have occurred otherwise than by a revolt. It wasn't unsporting really, as both crews got medals always, and no one thought anything of winning the race.

Adrian Ellison

But not every rowing tale is poetic. Some not even close.

This story is from Adrian Ellison, coxswain of the 1984 British Men's Coxed-Four containing Martin Cross, Richard Budgett, Andy Holmes, and Steve Redgrave.

After surviving the experience described below, their boat went on the win the Olympic final on Lake Casitas, Great Britain's first rowing Gold Medal in thirty-six years.

The current era of British rowing success began with this boat. Rowing is the only GB sport to have won at least one Olympic Gold in every Games since 1984.

Bub-bub-bubub

Once we heard that there was going to be a boycott of the 1984 Olympics in Los Angeles, I think it was [British Director of Coaching] Penny Chuter who arranged specially for us to race at Berlin-Grünau in East Germany prior to the Games to get the opportunity to race against the Eastern Bloc teams.

We had to use a borrowed VEB shell with borrowed blades, and it may just have been pure coincidence, but the boat was way too small for us and we couldn't adjust the gearing on the blades at all. It was all quite unsuitable, but it was all that we had.

We were racing on the course where they had held the 1936 Olympic Regatta, and the water got rougher and rougher as we headed towards the start. We had to stop halfway up to avoid a deer swimming across the lake. Soon the boat had picked up so much water that we had to find somewhere to go and empty it out. I spotted a beach over on the far side, so we headed for that. Everybody got out. We tipped all the water out, got back in... and then realised we were in the middle of a nudist beach.

We turned around and paddled another 500 metres to the start, by which time the boat was full of water again, and because I'm lying down in the bow of the boat, as soon as the race started the water was sloshing up and down and I was getting drenched on every stroke. All I could hear behind me was the crew just laughing their heads off. The reason was because I was talking to them through submerged loudspeakers, and all they could hear is, "Bub-bub-bubub. Bub-bub-bubub."

I've never ever been in a race like it. There was no way we were going to win. I think we came third behind the East Germans and Russians, but everybody just treated it as the joke it was. For about seven minutes I was more or less getting drowned every stroke, but never have I been in a funnier situation in my life.

Jeff Klepacki and Jamie Koven

The coach of Adrian Ellison's 1984 British Olympic Champion Coxed-Four was Mike Spracklen, who grew up in Marlow, England. Here are Americans Jeff Klepacki and Jamie Koven discussing Mike, who was their coach as they prepared for the men's eights competition at the 1994 World Championships, which they won for the United States.

I *AM* a World Champion!

Klepacki: In the end, what Mike Spracklen gave me wasn't really so much the technical aspects of rowing but more a psychological approach to the sport. He's a master at psychological empowerment, where every day the way you carry yourself, the way you eat a meal, the way you show up on time, the way you care for your equipment, the way you put the boat in the water, the way you paddle from the dock, you do it as if you were already a World Champion... and nothing less was acceptable.

You'd think practice was over. Practice *wasn't* over until the boat was in the boat bay and you were on your way into the shower. If guys were screwing around and you had a poor paddle back to the dock, he'd make you stop and say, "Is that the way a World Champion would paddle back to the dock? Why don't you rethink that and do it again?"

Koven: With Spracklen, in everything that we did, we had to be acting like a champion, trying to do it the best we possibly could. That was understandable on the water during timed pieces, but some days we would play

Frisbee football instead of going on the water. We'd have to run laps around the soccer field first, and I remember guys cutting the corner, and Mike got just furious. "While cutting corners has nothing to do with rowing, you are *clearly* not acting like champions."

That was the mindset. *Everything* that you did, you had to do it as well as you possibly could.

Klepacki: These things may sound like minutiae, but when they are instilled in you hour after hour, day in, day out, week after week, through ten months of the year and you're at the first regatta and you face your competition, you actually walk, talk, look and *feel* like a World Champion. Maybe that's a tenth of a second, and maybe that's the difference.

I thought I already had the conditioning and the technique, but thanks to Mike, I was finally ready to win psychologically, if that statement means anything. It wasn't until the Spracklen era that I could say, "I *know* I can win this race. I *AM* a World Champion!" It was a completely different mindset for me.

Don Breitenberg

In the wake of the success of the best-selling *The Boys in the Boat*, there is much interest in American Al Ulbrickson, longtime coach of the University of Washington.

In the spring of 1941, young Don Breitenberg was rowing for Lane Tech High School in Chicago, Illinois, when the Washington Huskies stopped off during their annual three-day 3,000-mile train trip from Seattle, Washington on the American West Coast, to Poughkeepsie, New York on the American East Coast, for the Intercollegiate Rowing Association Championships. Don watched them practice on Lincoln Park Lagoon.

A Man of Few Words

I had never seen anything as beautiful as those white blades in perfect coordination. Right then and there I determined to row for the UW.

But World War II intervened. While serving in Europe as a paratrooper in the 101st Airborne, I periodically wrote Coach Ulbrickson from the war front. He hand-wrote letters in response, and I carried them around in my helmet for years until they finally disintegrated.

At the end of the war, I hitchhiked to Seattle, and when I finally met Al Ulbrickson in person, he merely said, 'Well, you finally made it.'

Duncan Holland

Born in Britain but raised in New Zealand, Duncan Holland has coached at the national team level in Netherlands, Switzerland and New Zealand. He coached Cambridge in the Boat Race between 2006 and 2008, but his rowing tale is about a dear old friend.

And Waikato are Sprinting!

Karapiro-Auckland Champs 1970, '71 maybe. Youth eights. My Hawkes Bay against Waikato.

Coming through the 1750, we were leading them, had about two feet, as we used to say in those days.

Pete Badley – the late, great Pete Badley – was commentating. I could hear him saying, "And Waikato are sprinting! And Waikato are sprinting! And Waikato are sprinting!" Waikato being Pete's club, of course.

Boris Starling

Harry Mahon coached for his native New Zealand, Switzerland, South Africa and Great Britain. Here is a reminiscence from Boris Starling, a *New York Times* bestselling crime novelist and Eton old boy.

Harry's Last Chance

Harry Mahon was perhaps the greatest rowing coach in history. He regarded the quest for the perfect stroke not just as a technical matter but as something deeper – the flow of existence, perhaps. Listen to the boat, he'd tell his charges.

Hear the boat sing.[7]

He'd coached all over the world and at every level, from schoolkids to internationals, and his crews had won pretty much every prize going... bar one. He'd never won an Olympic Gold in the blue riband event, the men's eights. Olympic men's eights are all technicolour, sound and fury: they go fast enough to pull a waterskier.

Sydney 2000 was Harry's last chance, not because he was retiring, but because he was dying. He had liver cancer, and there were only so many times the chemo could keep it at bay.

Along with Martin McElroy, he'd taken charge of the British eight, and it didn't seem at first as though they stood much chance. Where other nations had stacked

---

[7] From *The Oarsman's Song* by Steve Fairbairn.

their eights with the best rowers – particularly the U.S., world champions for the past three years – the Brits had gone the other way.

Their flagship boat was their men's coxless-four, in which Steve Redgrave was soon to win his fifth Gold and a knighthood. Next came their men's pair. The eight was for the also-rans. Whereas Redgrave & Co. trained in relative luxury at Henley, the eight worked out of a dingy gym in Hammersmith. Whereas Redgrave had the BBC documentary *Gold Fever*, the eight had to resort to public fundraising to afford a new boat.

Not that it did them much good to start with. In their heat, they were beautiful to look at – Harry's crews always were – but they had no bite, no aggression. They finished second to Australia, meaning they'd have to go through another round to make the final. They paddled over to the pontoon where Harry and Martin were waiting. Harry pointed into the distance.

'Boys,' he said simply, 'dressage is 40k that way.'

They were much better in the repêchage and got a decent lane for the final. The night before the biggest race of their lives, they discussed tactics. Conventional wisdom is to treat the 2000m in three separate blocks – get out fast for the first 500, settle into a rhythm for the middle 1000 and then wind it up in the last 500.

They decided to do it differently. They were going to go out fast and keep it there, daring the others to come with them. It was insane: the human body can't sprint for five minutes. It just can't.

But they also knew that at some deeper level, where Harry always encouraged his rowers to go. Olympic finals were won and lost by the crew who would hold their hands to the fire the longest.

Finals day dawned bright and warm, a perfect Sydney spring morning. On the Lake Penrith startline, cox

Rowley Douglas said, 'If I have eight men who will in the next few minutes show the kind of spirit and commitment which Harry shows every day of his life, we'll win this thing. Do I have those men? Show me that I do.'

They leapt from the start as though possessed. Quarter of a length up at 500, three-quarters of a length by 1000. If they could get clear water, it would be all over. No one could make up that margin.

But strive as they might, the gap was still three-quarters of a length as they reached the last 500. Not enough to be sure.

Not quite enough.

And now the charge began. The U.S., unable to live with the white heat of the occasion, were gone. Croatia, all beards and Balkan brio, threatened briefly before fading. It was the boat right next to the Brits who were closing the quickest. Green and gold. The Aussies on home water hunting the Poms[8]. Always a bit of spice when those two are involved.

The noise from the stands reverberated across Penrith in pressure waves. Stroke Steve Trapmore was no more than three feet from Douglas at frontstops, but he couldn't hear a word above the din. The Aussies were taking back a man every three or four strokes. Through the double vision of their exhaustion, the British boys saw the lane markers change colour. Only 100m to go. The line was coming.

Sanctuary... if only they could get there.

---

[8] In the far reaches of the British Commonwealth: South Africa, New Zealand and especially Australia, "Pom" is a slang pejorative term for Englishman. A shortening of "pomegranate" – which sort of rhymes with immigrant – with additional reference to the fact that the harsh Australian sun could turn British immigrants' skin pomegranate red.

Another 10 strokes and the Aussies would have had them... but they'd run out of water. The Brits were home by less than a second. As they skidded to a halt, Douglas was nowhere to be seen. He'd leapt from the boat in sheer ecstasy the moment they crossed the line.

They never rowed again as a crew. Most went into business. A couple became teachers. Trapmore now coaches the Cambridge blue boat. They're not famous or feted, but they're no less special for that. On that morning, with the total trust they placed in each other, with the knowledge that they held in their hands not just their own dreams but the dreams of all the others, too, they were kings of the world.

They received nine Golds, one each for the oarsmen and the cox. Coaches, rather unfairly perhaps, don't get medals. But Harry didn't need one. He, and they, knew what he'd done.

Harry Mahon passed away nine months later.

Alistair Potts

Another reminiscence involving Harry Mahon.

Coxswain **Alistair Potts** steered the winning Cambridge Blue Boat in 1998. He's also a Henley winner, Head of the River for Trinity Hall, and 2000 World Champion for Great Britain in the men's coxed-fours.

The Talented and Curious Mr. Ripley

So this is September '97, and we're all getting ready for another Boat Race. We've got some big new names in the squad, but it is the curious Mr. Ripley who sticks out more than all.

Imagine if Björn Borg joined your rowing team. Or Jack Nicklaus. Or Jimmy Connors. Same sort of thing. Andy Ripley's forty-nine years old, but he's a rugby super-hero who afterwards found fame on the BBC's SuperStars programme, which was basically about being hard: squat jumps, cycling, swimming and running like an idiot, that sort of thing.

Only the thing is we don't really *know* Andy Ripley. We're all too young.

Or German. Or American. Most of the Cambridge squad are less than half his age, and he's a pretty unorthodox physical type for a rower. He's a rugby forward. I guess the coaches know him better, but he's older than them as well.

So we start off with all the physiological tests in the gym, which involve weights and ergs and lactate tolerance and pull-ups, and Andy's mostly middle of the pack of about 35 contenders, maybe a bit above average. But then we do peak power on the erg, which is a bit of a laugh. Six strokes see how low you can split. I don't remember the results, but I remember hoping that someone would go under 1:00. No one did. What I *do* remember is that Andy, this huge quiet guy with crazy hair, comes in second. Out of everyone, Olympic medallists included!

And so things settle into their normal routine, and Andy just becomes one of the boys. He's not self-consciously trying to get down with the kids. He's just chatting and laughing and getting on with it, and very quickly everyone really forgets he's different (except when the press turn up). He's just one of the guys at the lower end of the squad trying to keep improving enough to survive the next round of chops. If I were he, I'd drive myself to Ely rather than sit in a rubbish minibus. But that isn't his style. Everyone likes him, but everyone's looking out for themselves, too.

The thing is Andy's really a novice at rowing. He's just been at it a year.

Of course he is strong as an ox. For an old bloke, he's unbelievable. At the erg championships he had been frustrated that he was a little short of his fiftieth birthday, which would have meant a different world record. I don't remember his time, but I do know he later set a WR in his fifties at 6:07.

So one Saturday between outings Robin [Williams] announces we have to watch one of his videos, which is pretty normal, so we all pile into the video room preparing for twenty minutes of gawping at ourselves and Robin saying bla-bla technique bla-bla pay attention bla-bla catch release bla-bla. He presses the play button, and we get... "Andy Ripley's Workout for MEN", which someone had picked up from a bargain bin for 99p or something. Complete with cheesy music. A good gag.

The writing is on the wall when Andy doesn't get selected for the two Trial 8s in December. But Harry [Mahon] has been really keen to get Andy rowing well. Harry would always spend an extra amount of time with any boat that Andy was in. I think he was really, really keen to see if he could get him up to scratch. I spend many hours in the coaching launch with Harry that winter. I'd be freezing to death, and Andy would be in some pretty awful quad, which just looks miserable on a cold winter day, but Harry would have them stop and do drills and stuff.

I think all the coaches want to keep Andy on, but they're pros, and they're fair, and they know it would be wrong on all fronts to cut him any slack when it comes to selection.

So they don't.

Now it's early January, and we've only been back from Spain for a short time. The way it works is that you all turn up every day, Robin reads out the crew lists, and it's pretty much mix-and-match with a good mixture of eights and fours and pairs. Only today he's reading off what's obviously an A crew, we've got Smith and Forster and Weber and Crombie and the rest of what would be the Blue Boat. I think Story is the only one not there. So Ripley fills his spot.

And we're psyched because this is the first time the (nearly) best eight have been out, and I'm thinking the coaches are trying a new idea to get Ripley rowing better by sticking him with the best possible people.

And it's an awesome January afternoon with no wind, no clouds, and the boys are rowing really well. We're coming home after an 22k outing, and we all know it's very good and we're excited because this is *the boat!*

It's late in the afternoon, maybe 5pm, and the water looks like oil. The only colours are deep purples and oranges and reds because the sun's almost gone. I remember it so clearly because I was thinking this is so strong, and we're going to go faster than any boat ever. I think everyone was so excited at what Robin and Harry had built, and wondered what Andy was thinking... because pretty much this was a good as it gets.

And I'm silent for a change because the coaching boat's gone off and all you can hear is the boat. I can see the Cathedral, which is the only thing you ever see at Ely, apart from cows and reeds, and the Cathedral is black against the purple sky. We're all thinking about the Race. And the boat is flying at twenty-two.

Of course it wasn't a strategy to improve Ripley at all, it was (in his own words) "a last cigarette offered to a condemned man". It was the only time the coaches did anything sentimental in all the time I was at Cambridge. Without wanting to sound too melodramatic, I think that was the last time I saw Andy. That's how it works. People just disappear. Andy did, that very evening.

Three months later, Andy wrote a great piece about his time with CUBC for the Boat Race programme. It said that after he was dropped, he went back to his college boat club to row on the Cam. And as he toiled with the rest of his crew, his cox would exhort: "Row like Andy".

No one had ever said that about him before.

When I read that, it made me smile. I like to think Harry smiled, too.

Charles Sweeney

U.S. masters rower Charles Sweeney of Capital Rowing Club in Washington, D.C., is well known for his social media posts about his life in shells.

Beige and Brown and Gold

I think I have a weird need to drag out any task or activity, even the most tedious, as long as it's just tangentially related to something I enjoy. It's like those endless dinners I serve at my place. I don't actually feel fulfilled unless I can spend hours dashing from specialty shop to farmers market to fish- and cheese-monger when – let's face it – Whole Foods Market actually has everything you need. And, though it drives Laura crazy, I even like standing around at 1am up to my elbows in suds and down to the dregs of whatever wine wasn't finished, listening to the Stones and doing dishes.

This is the only explanation I can think of for turning my road trip from Washington, DC, 400 miles north to Worcester, Massachusetts, for the 2017 U.S. Masters Nationals Rowing Championships into the ordeal it became.

Before the trip to Worcester became ridiculously slow, it went very fast. New Jersey takes a lot of guff, but I'll say one thing for the people of the Garden State: they know how to drive. My parents live in Georgia, and you'd think those good ol' boys would put the pedal to the metal whenever they hit the highway – Junior Johnson and Dale Earnhardt, *Smokey and the Bandit*,

Talladega, "Copperhead Road" and all that.[9] But you get on I-85 South out of Atlanta and you're lucky if the pickup in front of you is making 75, barely over the speed limit. On the other hand, if you get on the Jersey Turnpike at 7AM and you're not doing at least 80, you best get your ass out of the left lane or some deranged Piney[10] or bloodthirsty commuter will put you into a ditch.

Of course, I wasted all the time I made gunning the Hyundai up to the Big Apple at high speed by stopping for sweet summer peaches at the Union Square Greenmarket in Manhattan, for pizza in New Haven and getting caught up in an endless series of minor slowdowns. But I love driving and listening to rock and roll – it's my most American trait – so why not sit back, crank up the Grateful Dead, and enjoy the ride?

Fortunately – well, not exactly fortunately – the truck hauling the Capital Rowing Club trailer had broken down, and I got to Worcester in time to rig the boats – but not go out on the water, because conditions on Lake Quinsigamond were roughly comparable to the first day at the Rio Olympics, when a couple of boats almost swamped during the racing.

After rigging, I gave the coach a ride back to the hotel and discovered that I'd booked myself into a weird existential office park hellscape – not so much the middle of Nowhere, but the middle of Anywhere. A place with absolutely no sense of place, a brown and beige building set among brown and beige buildings, populated by beige people in subdued golf shirts and

---

[9] Probably too many cultural references here even for some Americans to follow. How to sum it up? Southern tradition of fast driving, going back to illegal moonshine smugglers during Prohibition.

[10] resident of the very rural New Jersey Pine Barrens.

beige khakis hauling laptops and rolie bags. Even the directions to the Doubletree Hilton Boston-Westborough – "Boston" my ass! Beantown is thirty miles down the Mass Pike from my room – are generic: Rt. 9 to Connector Road to Research Drive to Computer Drive to Technology Drive.

The carpet is beige and brown, the walls are beige and brown, and when you check in, they hand you a beige and brown chocolate chip cookie that has all the homey charm of any corporate gimme – a key chain, maybe – that's been sitting in a sanitary warmer behind the front desk since the kitchen defrosted it hours before.

The room is beige and brown and gray in all particulars, and the windows won't open so you have to breathe hotel air that smells of melancholy, basic cable and Legionnaire's Disease. In a sad attempt to convince you that you are actually someplace, the only things colorful in the hotel are the large photographs of downtown Boston they've scattered throughout – in my room I have two of Back Bay and one apparently of South Station. I remain unconvinced.

If Sisyphus were dead today instead of being condemned to ceaselessly roll a rock up hill, he'd spend eternity driving rental sedans to hotels like this, drinking cocktails with contrived names along with the all-male crowd in the Regatta Lounge before reviewing his PowerPoint presentation and dozing off in front of ESPN2.

I tried to give my room a little personality. I exploded my suitcase. There's nothing like a pile of rowing gear next to the bed and socks and t-shirts scattered on random horizontal surfaces to make me feel at home.

And there's the farmers market swag. In the entryway of Bouley Restaurant in Manhattan they put bushel baskets overflowing with Winesaps and Jonathans[11]. You walk in from the heat and stench and clamor of TriBeCa, and the smell of the apples transports you to an autumn afternoon in a Hudson Valley orchard. I'm hoping for the same effect in my room with the peaches and the tomatoes and the bread I've picked up. I'm also hoping that the room doesn't – instead of conjuring a Western Massachusetts farmhouse – start smelling like my kitchen after I've been away for the weekend and forgotten to take out the trash, and that I don't end up with a fruit fly infestation – one of the hazards of buying organic fruit.

The rowing, on the other hand, was going pretty well. On Thursday, the first day, I had one qualifying heat in the Men's Masters Eights, Class E (average age 55-59). Three boats would advance to the finals, and it pretty much ended up a solid workout rather than a real race, with us and our hated hometown arch-rival Potomac Boat Club pulling away from the pack at the start and coasting to a 1-2 finish.

They decided to heighten the tension for the E final by having us sit just beyond the start for 20 minutes or so, watching kind of a picturesque sunset over Lake Quinsigamond, listening to the soothing sounds of the traffic above on the bridge and, in my case, alternately obsessing over whether I was going to cost us the race through some obvious or subtle screw-up and whether or not we were going to make it back to the shore in time for me to get to a bathroom.

The race turned out to be a real barn-burner, with us catching Potomac at 500 meters and them trying to steal it back with a hundred meters to go. But we held those bastards off, and we are now – it's hard to say it with a

---

[11] varieties of apples.

straight face, but fun nevertheless – National Champions!

Beating our crosstown rivals by a second made it extra sweet. Everyone was high-fiving and laughing, even the guys who are usually pretty low-key or downright cantankerous. The coach, a dour Russian, was beaming, and people were dropping by to congratulate us.

It was a late race, and the sun had set by the time we finished re-rigging the boat, but I kind of didn't want to leave the parking lot. This was my first gold in a men's event – I had won in a mixed eight last year – and it came after five often-frustrating years on the water.

Even after we were done, standing in the almost-empty parking lot was like being in a club while they're putting the stools on the bar but you can still hear the echoes of the band you came to see, or smell the perfume of the girl you were dancing with, and you worry that if you go outside the magic will fade away.

On the drive home an immense full moon, the color of something Steve Redgrave might wear around his neck on an Olympic podium, rose over Bertucci's and Target and the Certified pre-owned Lexuses, the muffler places and Lab Corp. Back at the Doubletree, if you squinted – or maybe just lied to yourself – the moonlight seemed to turn even my brown and beige hotel a little golden.

My first race Saturday – the heat for the Men's Masters C Eights – 43-49 – may have been the prettiest race I rowed all season. Given my sub-par technical skills as an oarsman, I never thought a boat I was in could row that well. It kind of felt like a boat of destiny from the first stroke. During warmups we do "builds" – lifting the stroke rating gradually to get the muscles going and get a feel for what race pace will feel like –

and after the third one I nudged the guy in front of me and said, "If we row like that, we could win some races."

And sure enough...

I think we might even have been in fifth place after the start, not unusual for us, but we just ground the other guys down. By 500 meters it was a three-boat race, and we sprinted with uncommon elegance. We caught the last two boats with a hundred meters to go, beating the hated Potomac eight by .336 seconds and Riverside Boat Club from Cambridge, Massachusetts – always a tough crew – by .338 seconds. Only the heat, but a very satisfying race, and we finished with the fastest time overall.

The favorite in the final was going to be Cambridge Boat Club, which had a slower qualifying time than us, but they were not pressed in winning their heat. Cambridge tends to get rowers with the sort of pedigree that intimidates hacks like me – national team guys, former Harvardians and the like. It was pretty much assumed that they'd take the Gold in the final, leaving us with a reprise of the same three-way duel we'd fought in our heat that morning for the remaining medals.

And, it was another barn burner. Again we clawed our way to the front almost from the back. Riverside did us the favor of losing steam with 250 meters to go. According to Mikki, our cox'n, "It was beautiful to watch them just fucking collapse."

We rowed another lovely race, and we all rowed right up to the edge of complete exhaustion. As expected, Cambridge was three seconds up, but those bastards from Potomac turned it around and took the silver from us by .17 seconds.

The problem with a loss that close is that you feel – I feel, anyway – that I could have made the difference if I'd only rowed better or harder, that I could personally have made the boat go the eight one-hundredths of a percent faster it needed to go. I guess everyone feels that way, remembering a couple of bad strokes or wondering if you went into overdrive too early or too late, losing your power before the finish line or leaving something on the water.

You get the idea from watching sports on tv that if only you "give 110%" or turn in a "superhuman effort" you can always pull it out in the end by force of will.

This is not true.

Oh, well. The Potomac boat that we beat by three-tenths of a second two days ago? They have two Silvers now. We have a Bronze... and a Gold!

I'll take that.

Wanaka Rowing Club

What is it about rowing that turns us all into lifelong athletic supporters? Rob Bruce submitted the following from the private Facebook page of the Parents of the Junior Squad of Wanaka Rowing Club on the South Island of New Zealand.

Fifteen Reasons to be Grateful
Random Impressions from a Rowing Parent From a Small Rowing Club

1. Rowing is fun. Imagine learning to balance in a skinny boat that barely clears the water and then suddenly moves really, really fast. Now imagine being transported super-fast with only the sound of slapping water and gliding mountain scenery.
2. When you join up it doesn't matter where your fitness level is, and it doesn't matter whether you can catch or kick a ball. The only thing that matters is that you are committed to slowly building your fitness and honing your technique incrementally to enjoy the results in the months and years to come.
3. Imagine a true team sport. The team fails if it cannot work together and keep its rhythm. Your offspring will learn to respect and enjoy the company of others that they would not necessarily spend time with in ordinary life. They will bond over the importance of food before and after races.
4. Your rowing offspring will wake up in the mornings at times you never thought possible. In fact, teens can cast off their genetically programmed sleeping-in

gene, embrace the mornings and even comment that the early morning exercise helps them concentrate at school. You think I am lying... I am not. I have heard rowing teens talk about this in the back of my car. I was not hallucinating.

5. Your rowing offspring will say "it's not that cold" when you drop them off at the rowing shed when it's minus 4 degrees.[12] You go home and have a quiet nervous breakdown, but know that they always come back alive and kicking (and hungry, REALLY hungry).
6. Your offspring will embrace the wonder of New Zealand Merino[13] in the form of woollen socks that keep their warmth despite occasional sneaky bits of water negotiating past gumboots when getting into boats at the lake edge.
7. Parents quietly rejoice: teenage parties that go way too late are hard to mix with rowing practice the next day.
8. Your rowing offspring meet other rowers from other schools. They will meet all sorts... the beefy, the nerdy, the quiet ones (watch out), the bossy, the obsessive, the tall, the petite – to mention just a few. Fast rowers really do come in all shapes and sizes, and this blows the stereotype of the 'ripped' athlete to bits.
9. Rowing parents get to sit on the gorgeous grassy verges of stunning rivers and lakes, drink coffee and eat excellent bacon butties.[14] And then if you want to, you can bike along the lakeside to watch the

---

[12] 25° Farenheit.
[13] extremely soft and fine wool from the merino breed of sheep, originated in Spain but domesticated in Australia and New Zealand.
[14] Kiwi-speak for a sandwich, the key ingredients of which are bacon, butter and bread.

boats glide incomprehensibly fast as you marvel at the utter fabulousness of these wonderful young people.
10. You can stand at the finish line and scream like an idiot for your club's team, and no one bats on eyelid. No one cares that you are yelling like a madman at the water's edge. No one.
11. You learn that *www.rowit.co.nz*[15] is the best athlete database in New Zealand. Possibly in the world.
12. You learn of wonders of chocolate milk for recovery after your offspring's races. For your offspring... not you, silly... coffee is still the best recovery for extreme spectators.
13. You will be utterly grateful to the 'backwards' sport for the confidence it instils in your offspring and their team mates. You will get to watch these wonderful young people grow and develop. However, long drives to regattas involve an immersion into teenage music along with some snippets of gossip. This is good and bad; mostly good, but I have heard more K-Pop than I would ever want to in my life.
14. You marvel at the commitment and professionalism of the volunteering infrastructure that keeps the sport going. From camps mothers, to volunteer coaches, to school minivan drivers, to uniform organisers, to the wonderful old ladies manning the coffee and sandwich stands, to the race umpires and commentators...
15. You soon learn that you and they all have something in common, apart from rowing offspring. It is this: utter respect for this wonderful sport. It's a sport that

---

[15] the Regatta Central of New Zealand, indispensable website including results of local- and world-level races going back years.

enables young people to grow and develop in ways that many of them never thought possible.

Peter Mallory

This collection of rowing tales began with Charles Dickens and Herman Melville. The following contribution from your editor, American Peter Mallory, excerpted from his memoir, *An Out-of-Boat Experience*, references both authors, and to paraphrase *A Tale of Two Cities*, the day described below was the best of times, the worst of times.

Afterlife

On Friday, June 8, 1973, one of those indescribable late spring / early summer days in Philadelphia, I sit outside the boathouse and stare across the river. The sun has regained its strength, and the pungent smell of blooming flowers dulls my senses. Tree branches hang heavy with new foliage, and leaves rustle in the gentle breeze. The Schuylkill River oozes past Boathouse Row, and bugs buzz in lazy circles.

It's beautiful, but today I hardly notice, way too busy feeling sorry for myself.

"It is a damp, drizzly November in my soul."
Moby Dick, Herman Melville

The first year I coached, we lost two races during the season. The second year only one. This year we have finished undefeated... and yet we have come in second at the Eastern Sprints for the third year in a row! How could such things happen? I am overwhelmed by missed opportunities.

My kids have gone home for the summer, and I am alone... sitting on a bench overlooking the Penn docks, feeling as empty as the locker rooms upstairs...

The loneliest times of my coaching career have always come in the days after the rowing season has ended, and I am left without purpose in my life.

Some old guy in a suit walks by me, stops and stares out across the river.

Never seen him before. Businessman, distinguished, a touch of class in his stature. He's *really* old, probably in his forties, maybe six feet two inches tall, trim, maybe 180 pounds. I don't know.

He smiles...

I'm barely aware that he's talking to me.

Obviously a stranger... doesn't know anybody in town... came down to the river on a whim... he was a rower once, but considering his advanced age – is that *gray* hair at his temples?!!! – it must have been a *very* long time ago... not a Penn man, though... but did he mention he rowed for a while out of this very boathouse?

Interesting...

No... not really. I'm too busy rerowing my life.

Wait a minute!

Did he just say he wished he could go out for a row?

In a pair?

With me?

Does he think I'm out of my frickin' mind?

Come on! I wasn't born yesterday! Rowing in a good boat really *is* better than sex... but rowing in a bad boat is... well...

... and a pair worst of all!

The most unforgiving of all boats.

Not a "double," two athletes with two delicate sculling oars each. Easy, elegant, symmetrical. In French, *deux en couple*. As in "coop-le." Even sounds nice. I imagine Catherine Deneuve cooing in my ear, *"Voulez-vous ramer deux en couple avec moi ce soir?"*

"Avec moi? Mais, bien sûr!"

No. Not a double. No Catherine Deneuve. *Quel domage!*

A "pair," two athletes with one big, clunky sweep oar each, ungainly, one oar placed far in front of the other, asymmetrical, retarded. I imagine Madame Defarge looking up from her knitting, spitting tobacco juice on the Paris cobbles, pointing at me and passing judgment:

"Deux en pointe!"

She puts all her derision onto the final "t" sound, and it grates my ear as I am led to the tumbrels.

A pair.

God-awful boat to steer, to balance, to row.

God-awful.

If I end up in Hell, which seems a perfectly reasonable presumption on this particular day of my life, I fully expect to be directed to the bulletin board at the River Styx Boathouse, and if I'm *very* fortunate, I will be sent to the still-water tanks for a lifetime at steady state... or maybe I'll be chained to a noisy rowing machine with a handle studded with broken glass and the guy from the *Ben Hur* movie screaming and cracking his whip at me for the next thousand years.

That is, if I am very, *very* fortunate...

If I'm not... I'll be assigned to row in a pair with a total stranger.

Simple as that.

All this flashes through my mind as this lonely man with a kind face smiles down at me and suggests we go rowing... in a pair.

Him and *me?*

Him... and me... ?

What the Hell...

Literally.

Wouldn't this be the perfectly appropriate end to a perfectly horrible day in the midst of a perfectly horrible year?

I *deserve* this!

My mouth forms the words of acceptance as I listen, detached, from somewhere far above, from a great distance across the river.

His name is Dewey Something-or-other. Now what the Hell kind of first name is Dewey, anyway? We shake hands. (He has a firm grip, I notice.) I find Dewey some really dirty clothes in the lost-and-found box. We pick out a couple of oars and put them out on the dock. Get this. He has never even seen modern Mâcon blades close up before. Why am I not surprised?

We pick a coxless-pair off the rack, set it in the water, step in and push away.

Just like that.

As we sit and tie in, Dewey asks me what technique do I row. I look back over my shoulder and smugly tell him I can do them all: Conibear, Harvard, Wisconsin, Lake Washington, East German, West German, Russian, accelerated slide, steady slide, decelerated slide, explosive power, steady power, one hand, two hands, fast hands, slow hands, gradual roll, snap roll, no pause, pause at the catch, pause at the finish, I can do them ALL!

In short, I'm being a total and complete ass...

Nevertheless, soon we are gliding upriver deep in conversation and actually *doing* all those techniques.

And having fun.

You know, the boat feels okay for having some old fart in the bow-seat and my sorry ass at stroke.

Soon we are three miles up the river. We discover we actually have something in common. He tells me he had rowed at Stanford University, and Jimmy Beggs had been his coach. Gentleman Jim Beggs? Why, he had been my freshman coach here at Penn!

Is this a small world or what?

We swap affectionate stories. I never knew that Jimmy had coached at Stanford. I'm starting to figure out this Dewey guy is okay after all. The boat is flying, and I've never enjoyed myself so much.

We are just about back at the dock when he lets slip that he once actually rowed in a pair with Jimmy Beggs as his coxswain, so I guess that explains why our boat is going as well as it is. This guy has a little bit of experience...

Alright, I have to admit it. This has been downright wonderful. This is the best pair I have ever rowed in, maybe the best boat I ever rowed in...

Can you imagine?

Deux en pointe...

Wait a minute!

Where did you say you and Jim rowed your coxed-pair? Helsinki? As in 1952 Finland Olympics Helsinki?

That Helsinki?

Holy cow! I'm rowing with an Olympian!

Too soon we are back at the dock. Dewey is aglow. Magical afternoon. Can he buy me dinner? You bet he can! I want to hear more about Helsinki. I suggest Schnockey's Seafood House, a Philadelphia institution.

There we are in a booth sharing a huge pot of steamers, and Dewey continues his story. Seems their boat ran into some bad luck at the Olympics, but he and his partner – I never caught the other guy's name – they came away believing that they might actually have what it took to be competitive the next time.

My ears perk up.

"The next time?" I ask.

The *next* time?

Dewey continues. Trouble was that Jim Beggs was moving to Philadelphia to become the paid Freshman Coach at Penn. When they graduated from Stanford, Dewey and the other guy became Navy pilots, but they ended up being stationed 700 miles apart. So on weekends they would fly and meet somewhere so they could keep rowing.

They embarked on a four-year Olympic odyssey, this time in a coxless-pair, and coincidentally spending the last few weeks before the 1956 Trials rowing out of the Penn Boathouse while Beggsy gave them a final tune-up.

"So," I ask... "what happened?"

They went to Melbourne in 1956...

... and they won.

They *won?* The Olympics? I have just spent the day rowing a coxless-pair with an Olympic Coxless-Pairs Gold Medalist? I nearly faint.

I imagine dying... and somehow I'm going to Heaven after all. I go to the bulletin board at the boathouse along the river that flows through the Elysian Fields, and someone has put in a good word for me. I've been assigned to row in a pair with Duvall Hecht.

Afterlife is *good!*

Bruce Lodder

Sometimes it's who you know, especially in rowing, and not just Duvall Hecht. Bruce Lodder of Auckland Rowing Club was a temporary member of the Rowing New Zealand staff.

One Telephone Call

I was the team manager for the New Zealand Junior Rowing Team for four years. During that time I experienced some extraordinary highs and lows, triumphs and disasters.

My first year as a manager was 2004. The team travelled from New Zealand to Barcelona in Spain for the World Championships at Banyoles. It was my first time being a manager of an international team, and so it was a matter of learning the job as it happened!

My learning began in the airport at Barcelona. While we were herding the rowers towards the buses that were taking us to our hotel, one of the coaches came up to me and asked, "Where's my bag?" Everybody looked for it, but it had been stolen from beside him while he was organising the athletes. He lost his passport, money and all of his hand luggage. It took many phone calls and trips to Barcelona to get a new passport before he could start the return trip home.

We all got onto the transport, and as we arrived at the hotel in Banyoles later that night we suddenly realised that I had made a terrible mistake – we had forgotten to collect the oars at the airport! In those days, we brought our own oars from New Zealand. Luckily for me, my brother and several members of my family had come to welcome and support us. We unloaded the rowers at the hotel, and my brother and I immediately got back into the vehicle and drove back two hours to the Barcelona airport. By the time we arrived there, it was 2am.

The airport was completely shut up and locked. We looked at each other and decided that the best course of action was to try and find a way into the back of the airport.

Driving around the perimeter, we found an unlocked gate and drove in. We reasoned that there were only a few places where the oars could be stored, and so we approached the warehouse buildings. It was our good fortune that the third one we looked inside had the oars – we could see them lying on the ground. I made a stirrup with my hand, and my brother jumped over the fence, ran into the building, picked up the oars and passed them to me over the fence. By 5 o'clock the next morning, the oars were at the hotel and all was well!!

My second year as team manager took us to the Junior World Championships in Brandenburg in the former East Germany.

Before the regatta started, it was explained to everyone that no coaching from speed boats on the lake was allowed. One of the athletes in the team that year was Emma Twigg. Her coach decided that this rule not apply to him, and so he rented a waterskiing launch from a local resident. I was horrified to see this huge motor boat ploughing down the lake powered by a giant engine putting up a wake nearly three feet high! Emma's coach was reclining in the boat, which was being driven by its owner.

Needless to say, I was summoned to meet the FISA authorities in the form of Matt Smith, the executive director. He said it had been very clearly explained that this was not allowed and told me that every New Zealand crew would receive a five-second time "yellow card" in the first race! I negotiated hard, explaining that this was one person disobeying rules, and that the whole team should not be penalised. He eventually relented. It later turned out to be fortuitous that Matt and I had become acquainted.

In 2005, that part of Germany was still quite noticeably different from the old West Germany. The first thing we noticed was the food – they eat a lot of typical European food such as red cabbage. Imagine my trouble trying to get young New Zealand athletes to eat that! So I had to organise alternative meals for the team.

During the regatta, one of the athletes became ill, and we left him to rest at the hotel. Partway through the day, I returned in the van to pick him up and bring him back to the regatta to watch the racing. As I drove down this very narrow cobbled street in Brandenburg, I suddenly realised that I was completely lost. I got to an intersection and looked left and right, trying to decide which way I should go to find our hotel. I stalled the vehicle and was struggling to restart the engine when, at that moment, a tram came down the cross-street. The driver was clearly irritated. He continued approaching and gently nudged the side of the minibus. He got out waving his arms and shouting angrily in German. I got out and tried to make it clear that I did not understand him. I was a tourist and I was lost.

Then the police arrived, and I was taken to the police station and put behind bars. I spoke no German, and the police didn't speak English. Luckily, a translator was found so that I could explain that I was visiting the city as part of the Junior World Rowing Championships. I was allowed to make one telephone call, and I asked them to ring the regatta. They phoned the rowing course and spoke to Matt Smith, my old friend!

Fortunately, he quickly grasped the situation and told the local police that my presence was essential for the smooth running of the regatta. The police acted swiftly. I was put into a police car and driven to the course at top speed with lights flashing and the siren wailing.

I had thought they would drop me at the entrance to the regatta. How wrong I was! They drove me right down to the pontoons at the water's edge, sirens continuing to blare, where I was greeted by the organising committee.

That was one hell of a way to make an entrance at a regatta!

Matt Langridge

Like the rest of us, Olympic Champions put their trousers on one leg at a time... or do they?

Matt Langridge, Olympic and World Gold Medallist rower for Great Britain, began his rowing career in Northwich in the County of Cheshire in the northwest of England.

Back to Front

In my second-ever national championship regatta, I was 15 and went to the singles final as the favourite, obviously a little bit nervous, all excited because I'd go in there and hopefully win the race and be a national champion.

I sat at the start line – it was Strathclyde Park – took three strokes and came off my seat. Obviously, bit of a panic, but I managed to get back on the seat. By this point everybody else had kind of disappeared. Luckily, I managed to get back into my rhythm. I was strong enough even though I had given everybody two lengths off the blocks, I was good enough just to catch everybody up and row through them.

Crossed the finishing line – obviously, relieved that although I'd fallen off my seat and messed up the start, I essentially got away with it and still managed to win the race.

Came into the pontoon to collect my Gold Medal, and basically, everyone from Northwich was there watching.

Everyone was kind of pointing and laughing. I was thinking, "Oh, God, they must have known that I'd fallen off my seat." I thought I'd gotten away with it, but I'm never going to hear the end of it.

It was only when I came down from the podium that somebody – I think my Mum – mentioned to me that, actually, the reason why everyone was laughing so much, the source of such great amusement, had been that I had my all-in-one[16] back to front.

I had stood on that podium, my *first-ever* national championship, *all* those people taking pictures of me, and my all-in-one was back to front.

---

[16] called a unisuit in some parts of the World.

Joe Burk

American Joe Burk was one of the greatest single scullers of the 20th century. He was odds-on favourite for the 1940 Olympic title, but World War II intervened. During the war, Joe captained one of the legendary American Patrol Torpedo (PT) boats in the Pacific, winning the Navy Star and Silver and Bronze stars.

Joe first rose to international rowing prominence in 1938 by winning the Diamond Sculls at the Henley Royal Regatta in dominating fashion. To put Joe's time into perspective, he broke a 33-year-old course record, and it only took *another* 26 years for his time to be eclipsed. Diamond Sculls winners didn't begin to consistently row under Joe's time until the late 1980s, half a century after Joe.

At the age of 91, Joe told me the story of how a momentary lapse in concentration combined with his strategy of even splits down the course meant he nearly didn't repeat his 1938 success in 1939.

Winning Smile

A funny thing happened my second year in the Diamond Sculls during the final against Roger Verey from [Akademicki Związek Sportowy[17] Krakow in] Poland. He had twice won the European Championships and was really quite a good sculler.

With the way I rowed, I just learned from long experience never to worry about what happened at the beginning of a race because I knew that I could keep just about the same speed all the way through.

---

[17] Academic Sports Association

So in my race with Verey, he went out and took a lead, and I caught up, oh, about halfway down the course.

There was a strong cross-wind that day, especially there at the halfway point. I knew that my stern post was pointed right at the start float, but I hadn't thought about the fact that the wind was blowing me over.

All of a sudden, Bang! I hit against an upright on the log boom.

Luckily, I didn't capsize. My oar was turned up square at the time, and it was knocked out of my hands. I grabbed ahold of it, but by that time, Verey was back ahead of me.

I thought, 'Boy! I'm *really* going to have to work now!' and I forgot all about pacing and just rowed as hard as I could.

I finally caught up to him, maybe a quarter-mile from the finish. I started to go by him, but it was just about all I could do to keep moving.

I knew he would look over at me, so as I began to go by, I turned my head and smiled at him as though there was nothing to it.

Immediately, he dropped back, and that's the way I was lucky to win that second Henley victory.

Tom Weil

Another story from a U.S. Navy veteran...

In the following tale, American Thomas E. Weil, rowing historian, author, founding member of Friends of Rowing History, trustee of the River & Rowing Museum in Henley, and the world's premier collector of rowing artifacts and memorabilia, describes his *annus memorabilis*.

The Summer of 1970

The late '60s and early '70s were a transitional time of great cultural and political upheaval in the United States, and rowing was in no way immune from the waves of change. The late spring and summer of 1970 was an interesting time in rowing history and transformative for me, providing many of my most memorable moments, in rowing and otherwise.

Towards the end of the 1970 spring season, two events rocked Yale University. Protests over the bombing of Cambodia as an extension of the Vietnam War led to the killing by National Guardsmen of four Kent State University students, provoking widespread unrest on campuses across the country. At the same time, large crowds of activists thronged the streets around Yale to decry the trial of Black Panther leader Bobby Seale on murder charges, leading to a virtual shutdown of the campus amid the arrival of National Guard soldiers and tanks.

What's a coach to do when the most important race of the year is about to take place amidst a virtual military occupation? Our lightweight varsity and second varsity crews, the best that Yale had had in twenty years, were undefeated as we prepared for the Goldthwait Cup contest on Yale's waters against Harvard and Princeton. The night before the race, coach Jim Joy moved us to a motel outside the city. His precautions were for naught, as, the next day, both Yale boats beat Princeton, but fell to the Steve Gladstone-coached Harvard eights. And the unrest claimed another victim. When the varsity coxswain showed up in a Black Power T-shirt, he was switched with the junior varsity coxswain, not, as the coach made clear, for his views, but for introducing that distracting issue to the boathouse at that time.

Both our boats went into the Eastern Sprints seeded second. Both boats won their morning heats. Both boats finished second to Harvard in the afternoon finals. Traditionally, the winner of the Sprints goes to the Henley Royal Regatta, but Harvard, having gone to Henley the previous summer and having run the table in 1970 with a boat full of sophomores and juniors, took a pass at entering Henley's Thames Challenge Cup, which opened the door for us.

Except that another oarsman, Jon Van Amringe, and I, both Navy Reserve Officer Training Corps midshipmen, were to be commissioned as ensigns at graduation and sent to our assignments in the Pacific fleet. I explained to the senior NROTC officer that we needed our orders modified because our crew was going to England. The officer noted that I should have learned by now that one is expected to obey the orders that one receives. I pointed out to him that the orders were for Ensign Weil to report for duty, and that if those orders were not changed to allow us to race at Henley, I would flunk my finals, and the Navy would not have an ensign to assign. That argument appeared to have worked, because our orders were re-issued to place us on temporary duty, assigned to the NROTC unit over the summer, so that we could go to Henley.

Jon and I completed our coursework, and, on the appointed day, made our way to the campus auditorium where we were to be sworn in as naval officers, but that commissioning did not pass without incident. Prevailing anti-war sentiment was so strong that when our contingent arrived in full dress uniform, we found the building ringed by a cordon of policemen facing demonstrators trying to break in to disrupt the ceremony. The police opened a corridor for us to enter the building, and, although we could hear their shouts as we took our commissions, they were successful in keeping the protestors out.

An unprecedented circumstance gave us the opportunity to prepare for Henley at Gales Ferry on the Thames River at New London, Connecticut, Yale's training quarters for the Yale-Harvard boat race. For the first time in Yale rowing history, the freshmen heavyweight eight, which had had a miserable season, disbanded before the great rivalry contest. We moved into the heavyweight freshmen quarters at the Ferry and worked out with the heavyweight varsity and junior varsity before heading across the Atlantic.

Henley was, of course, an extraordinary experience. I had attended as a young spectator in 1963 and 1964, but it was very special to return as a competitor. We were one of four seeded crews, and met expectations by defeating Liverpool Victoria, a club eight, and then beating Garda Siochana, the Irish policemen, who were the defending Irish heavyweight national champions. Our run came to an end when we lost to the Leander Cadets in the semifinals, and watched them win the Thames Cup in the final.

The Garda invited us to come to Dublin and race in the Metropolitan Grand Challenge Cup, the Blue Riband of Irish fours rowing, the following weekend, and offered to host us for the trip. Upon arrival, we were plied with Guinness, food and more Guinness, to the point that we were barely able to stagger, much less row. The course at Lake Blessington was rocked by epic storms the next day as four of us raced to an honorable third, splashing along in a loaned wooden bathtub steered by a loaned 150lb Irish coxswain.

As we lay sprawled on the hillside overlooking the lake following the race, a spokesman from the Keble College, Oxford, eight clambered up the slope to explain that two of his crew were passed out in a local bar, and to ask whether two of us might join them for the race that was scheduled within the next hour. Two of us did, myself included.

The abysmal conditions had led to the course being shortened, with crews aligned for floating starts. Every time that a start seemed imminent, the Keble cox called to "draw even", whereupon all eight took a stroke to move the boat another length or two down the course. When the referees called for a halt to that practice, the coxswain raised his arm and shouted that there was a "wee" emergency, at which point the stroke stood up in his seat, and, in full view of the thousands of spectators on the hillside, dropped his pants and relieved himself over the side.

Of the race itself, I remember very little.

Back in the U.S., Jon and I reported for duty to the NROTC unit and were told that we were not welcome, as we would just distract the secretaries. Since our modified orders did not require us to show up at our new duty stations until the end of the summer, we were told that we could spend our time rowing.

Tony Johnson, the Yale heavyweight coach, had been asked by several non-Yale oarsmen to coach them over the summer of 1970. In order to provide them the opportunity to compete in that summer's regattas, Tony announced the formation of the New Haven Rowing Club and commenced training out of the Yale boathouse on the Housatonic River at Derby, Connecticut. Jon and I decided to race as a lightweight double under the same flag. While Tony's eight went their own way under his tutelage, Jon and I raced at the Royal Canadian Henley (my first doubles race), and then won the junior doubles title at the New England Amateur Rowing Association championships in Lowell, Massachusetts.

We entered for the elite lightweight doubles at the U.S. National Association of Amateur Oarsmen championships on the Cooper River in Camden, New Jersey, a six-boat final that included multiple national champion Larry Klecatsky and future world lightweight singles champion Bill Belden among our competition. A severe storm the night before had washed out the Albano-buoy course, so each of us had the unenviable task of navigating an unmarked 2,000 meters without fouling, colliding or running ashore.

Jon and I were still tying in when our race began. Figuring that there would be no re-start, we took off and pulled as hard as we could. The Klecatsky and Belden doubles, engaged in a fierce battle on the other side of the river and led the rest of us down the course until Larry's boat hit a drainage pipe, leaving Belden's double to claim victory. Protests swamped the officials table. It wasn't until we were placing our boat back on the car to return to New Haven that Tony came over, told us that we had finished second, and handed us our NAAO national championship silver medals.

We ended the summer traveling to St Catharines, Ontario, Canada, as spectators for the 1970 Worlds where we saw the lightweight eights exhibition race, a landmark for that class in FISA competition. We then both went off to serve on Navy destroyers with Vietnam deployments ahead of us. Jon concluded his service by coaching the Naval Academy lightweights, but that summer of 1970 provided not only the highlights of my racing career, but also my last days as a competitive oarsman.

Mike Davenport

American Mike Davenport recently retired after a long career of coaching men and women at the collegiate level, most recently at Washington College in Chestertown, Maryland. In the early 1990s, he also served on the U.S. National Team Staff.

Pan Am Trip

In 1991, I was boatman and rigger for the U.S. Pan American Rowing Team, responsible for all the rowing equipment. The competition site that year was in Havana, Cuba. It would be my first trip to Cuba, and I had concerns because relations between the two countries had been strained for 30 years.

The U.S. Olympic Committee leased a ship, the *Good Samaritan*, to transport our equipment to Havana. A few weeks before the event we left Tampa, Florida, loaded with shells, oars, and gear for other sports teams, and sailed for Havana.

Upon arrival, we were met by a great many Cubans from local rowing clubs. I was immediately impressed. They were kind and generous. Each rower treated our equipment as if it was their own as they loaded our boats onto their trailers and drove them to the regatta site.

The course, northwest of Havana, was beautiful. Each North and South American team had their own boat shed.

For the next many days, while waiting for our team to arrive, my job was to get the equipment and our area ready for competition. Whenever I needed help, such as moving boats, the Cubans would drop what they were doing to help.

The day prior to the U.S. Team's arrival, I was putting the finishing touches on our area. As I usually did on all of our international trips, I wanted to raise an American flag on a pole at the front of the boat shed.

I needed a ladder and asked Jose, a local rower I had befriended, if I could borrow one. I explained what I was attempting to do.

He nodded, left, and in a few minutes returned not just with the ladder, but with a dozen friends who wanted to help.

As we set up the ladder, the crowd grew.

I unfurled the flag. It was a good-sized flag, about six feet in width.

Upon seeing the flag, the crowd got excited. At first, I thought I might be doing something wrong. Was displaying an American flag upsetting to them? Was I "that guy," the insensitive American who would start a diplomatic incident?

Then Jose approached me, explaining (in English much better than my Spanish) that many wanted to raise the flag. It would be thrilling for them, not, as I had worried, an insult.

A rower was picked to go up the ladder. I gave him the flag, and up he went. As I held the ladder, the flag was unfurled.

When he came down, the crowd applauded.

Someone snapped a quick picture. Unfortunately, it really doesn't capture the true symbolism and feeling of the moment. Cubans, raising an American flag in Cuba in 1991!

That brief episode, along with the entire trip, impressed upon me the ability of sport, and especially *our* sport, rowing, to cut across cultural and political boundaries.

Drew Ginn

Today Drew Ginn is a three-time Olympic and five-time World Champion for Australia.
But he was the new kid on the block in 1996...

The Clarity of Calmness

This story goes way back, more than twenty years ago, at the Olympic Games in Atlanta. I was 21 years of age, the new bow-man in the Oarsome Foursome, Australia's defending Olympic Champion coxless-four. Me, a youngster getting a chance to break in – I apparently brought the average age of the crew down significantly! James Tomkins had coached me at school!... and now he was seated right in front of me.

We were sitting on the start line of the Olympic final, and I vividly remember looking across to the other crews and being extremely nervous. The Italian crew on the far side in Lane 2, the Slovenians just past them in 1, France and Great Britain in the middle, and the Romanians right next to us. They looked scary – Gold Medalist Dimitrie Popescu was sitting in the 3-seat of that boat. And all across the field there were other Olympic champion athletes, like the Searle Brothers in the British boat.

At the Luzern regatta, James had been steering from the 2-seat and struggling to get a word out, and so basically for the last thousand meters it was me who was saying "up", "go", "up, up", and we pulled the Italians back to 0.6 of a second on the finish line.

After Luzern, we had seven weeks to prepare, seven weeks to see if we could close up that margin and turn the tables. I was given the chance to call the race plan at the Olympics because I had showed that I was able to sit in the bow and just keep chattering all the way down the track. That gave me an immense amount of confidence.

So there I was, in Atlanta. The Olympic final.

The guys said it was all about getting out fast and staying relaxed, staying composed through the 500m mark, not about trying to keep up with the Italians or the Romanians. If they were going to do a flier, let them go, but no more than half a length. We knew that potentially Great Britain and the French crew might not be so fast at the start, so that would put us right in the middle of the field.

We got off to an "oarsome" start – pardon the pun. We went through 500, and I'm calling 'catches' and lots of breathing calls. Through the 750-meter mark, it's 'arms into the body', and 'keep the acceleration going'.

The guys had said that at the halfway mark if we were within half a length, they were confident that we could win. So I'm 21 years of age, sitting in the bow seat of the Oarsome Foursome... and we were within half a length at the 1,000-meter mark of the Olympic final! I thought, "I'll ad-lib here a little bit, I'll improv, and I'll give the guys a run-down of how we are actually tracking."

I have no idea why I got that in my head.

So I go, "Righty-ho, Italy, Romania half a length up, Slovenia, half a length down, France, Great Britain half a length down. We're in this, fellas! We are *in* this... "

And James turns round and says, "SHUT UP!"

... it was just like being back in my schoolboy eight with him in the speedboat going, "Righty-ho, Ginn, be quiet! Stop the talking in the 7-seat."

Having someone ten years my senior, James Tomkins, who had coached me at school, to have this life-long friend turn around over his shoulder *during the Olympic final* brought to me the clarity of calmness.

Our plan was that the 1,250-meter mark would be the start of our 'Gold Medal 500' – Put your foot down! It was just awesome to be able to make that call and feel the response. The confidence the guys had in me to take responsibility for that call, and to be able to deliver on that and to get the Gold Medal was exceptional...

But the key part for me, the awesome part for me, was to have those guys say afterwards that my enthusiasm had been a big motivating factor for them!

Mary Boland

Just like Drew Ginn, we all started at the bottom, and like Ginn, Mary Boland of Sydney University Boat Club in Australia has never forgotten her roots.

What's a Steering?

About fifteen years ago when I was a novice rower – I started rowing at 56 – my teammates and I learned to row in a quad that had – as I know now – no rudder.

In our first novice race, we borrowed a boat at the regatta. We launched, we started our race, and we wandered all over the course. It didn't matter because everyone else was ahead of us.

When we returned to shore, we said to ourselves, "Look, we row quite well, but we went just all over the course!" One of our more experienced club members asked us, "Well, was there something wrong with the steering?" We looked at him and said, "What's a steering?"

Ann Hewitt

Ann Hewitt, a member of Commercial Rowing Club in Brisbane, Australia, reminds us that we are citizens first and rowers second.

ANZAC Day

April 25, ANZAC Day, commemorates the Australia and New Zealand Army Corps and their fight against the Ottoman Empire at Gallipoli during World War I. We honour and encourage our children to honour current and past servicemen and women who fight for the freedom that we enjoy in our lands today. Within our rowing club, we have both Australians and New Zealanders.

A few weeks ago, one of the local rowing clubs put a call out to all the rowing clubs at our end of the river to ask if people would like to partake in a dawn service on ANZAC Day. Everybody answered the call beautifully, and there were about twenty boats out there – eights, quads and smaller boats.

We met at this particular point before dawn and had a minute of silence with the mist rising off the water. Then one of the coxswains read a poem about ANZACs, and someone blew a bugle call. The pink of the sun was just rising up.

Rory Gullan

Brit Rory Gullan has no background in rowing, but he has quite a tale to tell.

The Solo Sea to City Row

It's six weeks until I take on the first ever solo row 72km from the North Sea to the City of London in a Carl Douglas Racing Shell, in aid of Cancer Research UK and in my mother's memory. It's also three months since I first strapped myself into a single shell. I have to admit there is a small part of me that still questions why I would ever do such a thing.

Two years ago, my mother died, having fought cancer for 22 years. I say fought, but she actually seemed to take it in her stride gracefully and with a great deal of humour. Not many people knew she had cancer, as she didn't want it to be something that defined her, and it never did. Her attitude, which she instilled in my brothers and me in all we do, was that worry and stress don't particularly help any situation. The worst that could happen is failure. That's it. So why worry?

I carry this sentiment with me, and at times an unfortunate side effect of this is a stubborn determination to do whatever I've set my mind to. Take this underlying mindset and add to it a chain of events a year after my mother's death, and the idea of The Solo Sea to City Row was born.

We are all, unfortunately, affected by cancer. Whether it's ourselves or a relative, a friend or a colleague, it is something that resonates somewhere within all of us. My mother had such a strong character and handled everything with such apparent ease that despite having various forms of cancer for so many years, it was not something that controlled her life. As my brother put it best when he spoke at her funeral, she didn't lose a battle to cancer. She won. She lived an amazing life and is still with me in everything I do.

I wanted to celebrate this, set myself a huge challenge and raise money for Cancer Research UK, and although at the time I didn't know what I wanted to do, I knew it would have to be something that would test my mental and physical strength in a way that nothing had before. By chance, on a run along the Thames, I came across a sign for a charity that organises cross-channel rows. Having rowed in my first year at McGill University, Montreal, this resonated with me, and the decision was made. I would row the channel solo.

A chain of events then followed which moulded the idea into what it has become: the stark realization that my experience in rowing in a men's eight 14 years ago would only go so far in preparing me to row in a single, the ban on 'unorthodox crossings' by French authorities, and discussions with a different organisation about various other routes that might be possible, although none were recommended as a solo row in a racing shell.

I decided I would start my challenge at Southend Pier, where the Thames meets the North Sea, and finish in the City of London, a total distance of 72km. The challenge, in my mind, was not only the distance but also the reality of taking a fine racing shell into relatively open waters. Add to this tidal waters and unpredictable weather conditions, and enough people, rowers and non-rowers alike, telling me that it shouldn't be attempted, and I felt this was the right challenge for me. I met with

Cancer Research UK, set myself a £10,000 fundraising target, and got to work.

At the time I had no contacts in rowing and no access to a club or boat, so I started by contacting as many London-based rowing clubs as possible, asking for support. One club responded, and the response wasn't overly positive, but it was a start.

I was due to meet with the rowing club when I received a late-night email from someone on the committee who was emailing on behalf of himself, not the club, and who wanted to help. We spoke on the phone that night, and before long we had set a time the next morning to go sculling in his boat. His was the first positive feedback I had received from anyone in months, and it really struck a chord with me. It still does. He and his wife took me out on multiple sessions, gave me advice on technique, training, and kept me motivated. To this day I still think they don't quite realise how pivotal they have been to this row; this has all been possible thanks to people who simply wanted to help.

My girlfriend is the strong influence in my life. She will never quite understand just how supportive she has been to me and how much she has kept me going through the early mornings, sleepless nights, and, at times, injuries that have shaken my confidence. She has inspired me in the way she has done so much – all of it behind the scenes and unseen by others – and taken it upon herself to make my success in completing the row her responsibility as well.

Many have told me that what I'm doing is brave or inspiring, and I thank them for that, but really I just think I'm creating a common ground for a lot of other amazing people to raise a considerable sum for charity. The real inspiration is the overwhelming support that has been offered by so many people, both friends and strangers, and this continues to motivate me through my training.

As this is a relatively unprecedented challenge, I've based my training on multiple influences: strength training from my McGill rowing days, marathon training, discussions with ocean rowers, and simply getting on the erg and rowing time and time again. There has been a huge physical demand and as I get into the real long distances, both in the boat and on the erg, I'm beginning to realise the mental strain that comes with such a challenge.

While I will have a support boat with crew alongside me during the row itself, training solo on the water is, by definition, solitary. It is extremely solitary. Crews come and go for their training sessions, and three hours later I'm the only one left on the water. There is a wavering tension between the loneliness of the silence and the blissful peace that comes with it; I've yet to discover which will prevail.

I've learnt so much in the few months since announcing the challenge, I've met the most amazing and generous people, I've pushed myself harder than I ever have before, I've felt aches and pains in areas I didn't even know existed, and hopefully I've managed to maintain some level of humour over it all. I've rediscovered my love for rowing, and I know that will stay with me.

As for my mother, I know she would be proud. She would also probably tell me to stop making such a fuss and just get on with it.

Stuart Harrison

This story falls into the "couldn't-make-this-stuff-up!" category. In a previous era, the very politically incorrect Stuart Harrison, Harry to his teammates, rowed for Tailem Bend Rowing Club in Australia.

Oh, *That* Pair!!

Three local clubs around Adelaide in South Australia have gotten together to row under one club colour – in the wrong grades, of course, as there was no such thing as computer records back then – in the annual Easter Regattas at Mildura and Wentworth, about 200 miles away.

To do this we need to borrow a boat trailer. I arrange to use Adelaide High School's new trailer, go to pick it up and find it locked in the cricket practice nets. The rowing master, Mister Smith (not an alias), has forgotten to unlock the nets, and no one can be found to help. The old trailer isn't locked up, so I grab that and head off to Murray Bridge to load the boats.

We get all the boats loaded up in the dark and do the light check to find the trailer has ONE central red tail/number plate light. Lots of swearing and time to PANIC, as we are going to Mexico (Victoria) across the border and the cops are a little hotter on being legal over there.

The boys are pretty handy, so in the dark we start putting indicators and taillights on the trailer. This takes a little longer than normal as the rowing club bar is open.

So with lights fitted and way behind our tee-off time, we head out. First stop is the Wambi Pub, about an hour and half away. It's the only pub in the middle of nowhere in what used to be a railways gangers' town. We are just into our first pint, and a couple of young [sheep] shearers full of rum are starting to give us a hard time. Luckily for them, Lieske and Cooche, the owners of the pub, have been very generous to us over the years, opening the pub for us when we were going past or slipping us in the back door to grab a carton of roadies[18], so we depart in order to avoid an incident, and the shearers getting their arses kicked. We decide to camp at the border, about an hour away.

As we approach the border we can see lights, which is most unusual as it isn't a lit area. The closer we get the brighter it gets. Then there is this boom, boom, boom getting louder and louder as we get closer. We hit the border, and there are camp fires everywhere, flood lights and generators and music, really, really *loud* music, coming from the back of trucks and motor bikes – not just any motor bikes. *Harley-Davidson* motor bikes – and bodies lying everywhere around the fires. Insert some swearing. The Hell's Angels Motor Bike Gang are camped there.

No choice. Mildura, here we come.

We roll into Mildura Rowing Club at 4:30am on Good Friday. Within five minutes this Ford F350 pulls up next to us with a sleeper cab and towing a heavily loaded boat trailer. The door opens on the dog box, and all these empty beer cans start pouring out onto the grass,

---

[18] A cardboard container containing 6 . . or 12 . . . or even 24 (!) cans of beer intended to be consumed "on the road." Seriously?

followed by four very drunk rowers. Essendon Rowing Club has arrived. Buried under the beer cans is my mate Nick – better known as 'Nicorette' – who I have raced lightweights against many times. Sadly, he passed away a few Easters later. Time for more beers with Nico.

So as the sun rises we head downstream to find a camp spot on the river flats. By 11am we are all pretty well passed out from alcohol and lack of sleep. At some stage late in the afternoon, we start to come to life only to find that Dave is resting on a bull ants' nest. Several kicks in the ribs later, he murmurs that he knows. So as long as he knows, he must be okay, so we leave him there.

He doesn't look too good the next day covered in welts.

Saturday morning, and Frank has arisen with a sprained ankle. He had fallen down the grader bank on the side of the road and then passed out in his swag. The girls decide to take him up to the hospital as we head off to the regatta.

Some nine hours later, the Mildura Regatta has finished and Frank is still at the hospital, so nothing else to do but grab the eskies[19] and head to the hospital. We make ourselves comfortable in the waiting room. The nurses want to know what we are doing there and tell us we really should leave, but we say we are not going anywhere till Frank is fixed up. So when it becomes clear we are not leaving without Frank, he immediately gets his ankle x-rayed, strapped up and shoved out the door. He tells us that every time they were about to see him, another car accident happened and he'd get forgotten about. The National Street Hot Road Show was on at Mildura, which was just car prang after car prang.

---

[19] coolers for beer.

Sunday morning early, and Tractor steps on a chop bone which goes straight into the ball of his foot. No amount of pulling with a pair of tweezers is getting it out. As there is a hospital at Wentworth, our next stop, he decides to wait till Monday to get it looked at. Back on the piss.

At the Wentworth Regatta, we head off for our eights race, and we have a little honey named Jane from Power House, Victoria, pulling the strings for us. Jane is one of the few coxswains on my "Who Can Cox" list. We are sitting at the start line waiting for Essendon. Frank's up in bow-seat and I'm in stroke-seat, and I hear a bit of grumblin' from the pointy end of the boat. Frank has let one rip. Four days of beers and chops have caught up. By now, 3 is grumbling, then 4, then 5 then 6, and I take a deep breath. Poor Jane has tears rolling down her face, and she starts ripping into me. "You dirty rotten stinkin' bastard!" No amount of pleading could convince her it wasn't me.

By now Essendon have pulled up alongside and have grabbed their toggle. They start abusing each other. The umpires come past in their boat, and they are abusing each other. The umpire on the bank yells out, 'Crews, are you ready?' and Geoff up in our 3-seat yells out "No, we can't breathe!" and the umpire yells back, "Race delayed five minutes," while he, too, is coughing and spluttering.

Frank in the bow-seat is killing himself laughing.

After the air clears, we eventually get the race away. Essendon does us by a canvas on the line, but then they had won the Australian Lightweight Eights title the week before. Not bad, as we were just a bunch of scrubbers from a few clubs that just got together and slipped on Murray Bridge Rowing Club tops for the weekend.

Monday comes around, and Tractor has headed off to the hospital, which is right opposite Wentworth Rowing Club. Tractor returns from the hospital after a few hours. They couldn't get the bone out with tweezers or forceps or pliers and had to go off and find a pointy pair of vice grips to pull it out. Damn impressive piece of chop... which he proudly displays upon his return.

So with the regattas over and the boats loaded, it is time to fire up the V8, and Wambi Pub, here we come! Leiske asks why we left early Thursday night, and, on hearing our explanation, is grateful we did.

But that's not *nearly* my best Wentworth Regatta story. Another Easter, and we are racing a novice four representing Railways, and Jane from Power House is coxing us again. We had won the day before at Mildura.

Over in Mexico (Victoria), in novice and beginners races they use these heavy, slow, fibreglass coxed barges they call "tub pairs" and "tub fours". In South Australia, we also use "regulation boats", but our boats are light and fast compared to theirs.

So in our race we head down the course in our own regulation wood racing four, and Jane's calling works us into the lead.

But Jane keeps yelling, and now it's, "Get me to the umpire's boat!" Umpire's boat??? We are in the lead, and what the #@$& IS SHE ON ABOUT?

And where is all this wash coming from?

I look around, and we are passing the umpire from the race ahead of us. Max from Wentworth RC is in the umpire's boat, and the look on his face is priceless. It is usually the umpire's boat passing *us!*

Then Jane is on us about getting up to the pair. "Pair? What friggin' pair??"

"Oh, *that* pair!!" We have caught the women's novice pairs race that started five minutes before us. Wentworth is only a five-lane course with a twin pillar bridge to get through and a bend on the finish line. Jane is heaving on the strings to get us through the bridge, and her lungs are in overdrive as one-by-one we row down the crews from the previous race.

By now we're going past the club rooms, the commentator is screaming, and the bank is just a roar of noise. Everyone is at the river's edge watching this regulation four motoring through all these women's pairs. The disappointing part is we lost the women's race by a foot on the line.

And to this day no one believes us when we tell them we came second in a women's novice pairs race while rowing in a man's novice four.

Jen Kilby

Good thing fellow Australian Jen Kilby wasn't racing Harry's boat from the last rowing tale!

It Still Counts

In my very first pairs race, we were about 50 metres from the finish line, and we could see that we were catching those who were first.

Unfortunately, I grunted a stroke, and my oar popped out of the gate. We flipped just a few metres out.

We were leading the boat in third by so much that we thought a moment about getting back in the boat, but there was not quite enough time.

Technically, you can swim the boat over, and it still counts.

We came second.

Kirsty Dunhill

I wonder how veteran Lake Karapiro coxswain Kirsty Dunhill might have handled Stuart Harrison. With many years of experience coxing and coaching at the New Zealand school, club and national levels, she also commentates at the New Zealand Nationals, Maadi Cup and World Masters Games.

Yes, You!

Let's talk race tactics.

I have coxed many men's senior eights, and it was always very competitive. Most of the way through the season, I would have done my homework and learned who the guys were in our main competitors because by then I would know who the top three were probably going to be, and they were going to be in the lanes beside you.

Looking out at the boat next to me, I would talk about someone in their 4-seat or 5-seat, saying out loud that they must be tiring and calling a move on them. Usually, these rowers could hear, so it wasn't very pleasant for them.

By Nationals, I'd be sure that my crew knew what was coming and were ready to come through for me. I'd wait until we were about 7- or 800m through, and then I'd actually call out the person's name. It might be Michael, it might be whatever the name is. When he looked out, I'd say, "Yes, you! *That's* who I'm talking about. This 10 is for *you!* Let's go!"

It just breaks their crew down, and you know that you've got at least five strokes up your sleeve to have a go at them.

Stan Pocock

If you ever took an art history class, probably the most significant rowing-related work of art you were asked to study was a painting in the Metropolitan Museum of Art in New York which Thomas Eakins named ***The Champion, Single Sculls*** when he painted it in 1871.

Sometime later, someone got the bright idea of renaming it ***Max Schmitt in a Single Scull***, committing the now all-too-common linguistic heresy of referring to the boat in which a single sculler rows as a "single scull" instead of a "single" or a "single shell." Years ago, the subject came up in a conversation I had with Stan Pocock, George's son and successor, born in America but steeped in the English tradition of watermanship, one of the last generation of traditional boat builders.

A "Scull" is an Oar

A "scull" is an oar used by a sculler, and never, ever a boat! The very first time I saw it used to describe a boat was in a letter from someone on the East Coast who wanted to order a "scull." In all innocence, I replied to ask for details, including whether he needed it for port or starboard.

I never got a response.

Eric Mahoney

Rowers can recognise each other by lots of clues, by how they walk, how they talk, how they carry themselves, and how they dress. You *used* to be able to spot the grease on the back of our calves, but now I am dating myself.

This is Kiwi Eric Mahoney, obviously and most assuredly a *non-rower*, reminiscing about a visit to Henley Royal Regatta many years ago.

Clutching at Straws

In 1976, I was residing in Holland Park, London, in a flat that was made up mainly of colonial outcasts from Australia, New Zealand, and one South African. In addition, we had a single token Englishman to mediate between our colonial outpost and the surrounding locals.

Henley Royal Regatta – along with the other major sporting events – came along, and our English flatmate was able to source a number of tickets to the Stewards' Enclosure.

On the day in question, much to the dismay of our English host, we arrived at Henley in shorts – boxer shorts, as a matter of fact – a t-shirt, and straw hat, what we would describe as appropriate attire for a trip to the local beach in New Zealand, our part of the world. We were simply not allowed to enter the Stewards' Enclosure.

Everyone else – the locals, of course – was appropriately attired in formal dress befitting an occasion such as the Henley Royal Regatta. We colonials were left to sit along the riverbank on a makeshift picnic rug, and we proceeded to drink beer from cans and eat pork pies as we watched the racing throughout the afternoon.

However, perhaps justice was seen to be done when, at the end of the regatta, a crew representing the Thames Tradesmen's Rowing Club scored an exceptional victory in the Grand Challenge Cup, the final event of the day. As it happened, the local supporters and members of Thames Tradesmen were so ecstatic about this outstanding achievement that they all rushed down to the pontoon that was in front of their pavilion, which, with the increased weight, gave way with a resounding crack and parted from the riverbank with about 30 or 40 of the locals – fully garbed with top hats and boaters – cast adrift into the middle of the river.

As the saying goes, "A drowning man clutches at straws."

The only thing afloat nearby was in fact the Thames Tradesmen's eight-oared shell, and, of course, as these esteemed members scrambled aboard, they ended up, shell and all, submerged in the river and floating past our little colonial encampment some hundred metres downstream.

We gave them a resounding cheer of best wishes.

Tina Duff-Dobson

It's not always Stewards' Enclosure attire for rowers. All too often it's a lucky hat, which inevitably deteriorates over time.

And no matter who you are or how careful you are, if you row long enough, you are going to end up in the water at a most inopportune moment, as Kiwi Tina Duff-Dobson discovered.

Manky Old Cap

It was the middle of winter – freezing cold – here on Lake Karapiro, and I was out rowing a double with a friend who's very, very experienced, and had never, *ever* tipped out of a shell.

He wears the mankiest of caps, and this day his manky old cap blows off, so he says, "I've got to go back and get it."

We back over it. He's a lot bigger than me, a lot more capable than me, and he leans over the side to get his cap which has now sunk to the bottom.

In we go. So, we had to swim to shore through the weed, take the oars out, empty the boat, get back in, and row another 5K back home against a cold southerly wind.

And this gentleman – he shall remain nameless – had never fallen out of a double before... but he did with me.

His response? "Weren't you balancing the boat?"

Tonia Williams

This tale is in the "don't-try-this-at-home-or-anywhere-else-either" category. Despite the following shenanigans, Tonia Williams of Great Britain and her women's lightweight coxless-four teammates came second at the 1992 Worlds and first in 1993.

He Didn't Like Me

Talking about rowers' injuries before significant competition, we were traveling to the 1992 Lightweight Worlds in Montreal – same year as the Banyoles Olympics so, lightweights and juniors had separate Worlds from the fat-weights, as we used to call them. Our boats were being shipped separately because we had a training camp ahead of the main team at the Craftsbury Sculling Center in Vermont, USA, which was fabulous, but dynamite[20] for lightweights because the homemade peanut butter was to die for. When you're trying to come into competition weight, that's not much fun. But we got there a few days ahead of the trailer and Billy, our coach, and we had to occupy ourselves and kind of break it up a bit.

Craftsbury is kind of out in the wops, just a little bit rural. And so, alternative activities were required. We did ALL the things that you really should do coming into the world championships as bony, dieting women. We went for a horse ride, and we went for a bike ride.

Both were quite adventurous.

---

[20] as in bad.

So, the horse ride was first, and the four of us duly hopped on some horses and went for a little trek through the woods. The group got split. I can't remember the sequence of events, but, anyway, I ended up bouncing out of my horse's saddle because he didn't like me. I picked myself back up, got back on the horse, and then heard this scream from behind me. My 3-seat was in a heap on the ground. She'd also been thrown by her mount, so we go, "Hmm... Billy will be well impressed!"

It was kind of check all over for no breakages. Right. Get back on and carry on back to the stables.

And then, the next day, we decided to jump on mountain bikes. Fortunately there were no misadventures, but, you know, you talk about stupid things to do when you're on tour and waiting for rowing boats. It's like there's only so much sitting around looking at water that you can do.

Chelsea Dommert

American Chelsea Dommert began her coxing career in Chattanooga, Tennessee, before moving to Miami, Florida. She is author of *Coaching the Coxswain*, Coaching Blog of the Year in 2012. Names have been changed to protect the innocent.

The Storm

It was a dark and stormy night...

That's a lie. It was a typical muggy, hazy afternoon in the customarily-hot city of Miami, Florida. A Wednesday, to be specific – my day off. The women's rowing team I coached did not practice on Wednesdays. I was pedaling my bike down some street without a sidewalk when I received a text message.

It was the men's assistant coach, Magnanimo (not his real name, but close). Their coxswain needed to recover from surgery, so he wanted to know if I could cox the boys today. Sure, why not? If they can't practice otherwise, it's practically an obligation. I switched to my weather app to see what sort of conditions I'd be dealing with. It said sunny until evening when a storm would roll in. We would get off the water well before evening, though, so everything seemed copacetic.

I steered my bicycle southward to go cox high school boys for the afternoon.

We headed out onto the water with Magnanimo at bow-oar and one of the girls (who came to practice just because she felt like it) rowing at 2.

Now here's the thing about Biscayne Bay, where we rowed: to get to calm water in one of the man-made yacht passages, first you have to cross about 2,000m of open ocean. Annoying... but bearable as long as the weather doesn't flare up.

On this particular day, we crossed the bay without incident and held practice in the waterway. We did 500m pieces, and we finished an hour's worth of work before heading back. When it was time to go home, we left the shelter of the yacht passage and headed back into the bay.

Magnanimo wanted to do one last 500m piece on the way home, but within 60 seconds of entering the bay, the sky suddenly turned an angry black, and we could feel the wind beginning to pick up. Next thing we knew, the rain had begun, and the waves around us grew larger and larger. They started sloshing into the boat.

Larger.

And larger.

My stroke-oar announced, "It's okay – our boat is self-bailing."

Larger.

And larger.

The rain started to pour. We hadn't moved forward at all since we got into the bay.

It got worse.

I tried to get parallel to the waves, which was laughable because they crested at about my shoulders, and no finagling could stop 'em crashing over our boat. Our boat filled with water. FAST. I said something to Magnanimo over the box, but the box suddenly wouldn't amplify. I looked down. The box was completely underwater. The speakers were underwater, too. Moments later, the water was approaching our gunwales.

Magnanimo and I decided to abandon our plan to conduct a 500m piece. We had to get the kids out of there stat. Maybe sixty meters to our port side, a high concrete seawall with wooden yacht docks rose out of the water. It was the best option. We turned and rowed by a pair toward the edge.

It only took a few strokes. The wind and current had picked up fast, and now we were drifting at breakneck speed toward the yacht docks. Magnanimo picked a dock and jumped out of the boat to swim over to it. He climbed onto the dock, which sat maybe 30 inches above the water. As we drifted closer, he held us off the dock in the bow, removed his oar, and started dragging the 2-oar up onto the dock, too. The waves were only getting bigger.

As this happened, our stern swung menacingly toward a particularly vicious concrete portion of the dock. There was no way we wouldn't hit it, so I jumped out of the boat and swam over to it so I could hold the boat away. The water was about five feet deep there, but my feet found a piece of coral to stand on so I could stabilize my 5'4" self while I held off the dock with my left hand and the boat with my right hand, with my body in between. Thank goodness there was no lightning – just wind, waves, and rain.

One by one, we got the kids off the boat and pulled out their oars. They all got up onto the dock and piled their oars behind them. We made them sit up there, three feet above us, out of the waves. Magnanimo dipped back into the water to hold the bow of the boat off the dock while I held the stern. I placed both of my hands on one of the pilings supporting the dock and locked out my arms, letting the boat buck against my back. The rain continued to pour.

Right now, you all think I'm lying. I'm totally not.

This lasted maybe ten minutes. The kids remained on the dock. The girl was crying because she had gotten a cut and the salt water had gotten into it. The 6-oar kept bellowing, "Why didn't anyone bring a CAMERA?!?!?!"

"Shut up, Andrew. Shut. Up."

Finally, the wind and rain died down, the sky cleared as fast as it had darkened in the first place, and the sea returned to a relative calm. We had to figure out a way to get home, so we bailed the boat as much as possible by turning it sideways in the water and lifting it up. We set it back down, put in all the oars, and made the kids go next to their seats to try to launch. In went middle-four, then stern-pair. I hopped in. Bow-pair went last. Magnanimo wanted to swim us away from the dock so we would be pointed away from it. As he hopped in and the bow swung away, though, the current pushed our stern forcefully back toward the dock. So I jumped back out to push us away again.

That's when Magnanimo decided to start rowing by pairs.

Keep in mind, I was not in the boat at this point – I was just hanging onto the gunwale and being dragged along. Stroke-oar tried to help, but he could hardly move he was laughing so hard. It's not so tough to hold on by pairs, anyway. I yelled at Magnanimo to stop, but he couldn't hear his boxless, drowning coxswain over the roar of the ocean. Then he called the boat to row by bow-six. I was still just getting dragged along like a half-unseated cowboy on a bucking bronco. I hung on for dear life during the drives, and I tried to scramble back into the boat on the recoveries. Over and over. It wasn't working. At all. I made stroke-oar yell out to the bow, and he finally contained his convulsions enough to do so.

FINALLY, the rowers stopped. I flopped my way back into the boat, exhausted, spitting, and struggling not to curse. I climbed onto the two gunwales on all fours, gasping for air and whispering over and over, "Magnanimo... I will kill you... Magnanimo... I will kill you... " and every single one of the boys bent double with laughter.

We were all in the boat once more. We still had a 500-meter piece to do, but it was more of a "haul tail back to the dock so no one figures out what happened" piece.

We docked two minutes before the official end of practice.

We figured we would be best off not explaining this to the boss-man, so once we put the boat away, we walked into the erg room and reported technical difficulties as the reason for our tardiness. As Magnanimo said this, the 3-oar put his hand to his hair and crunched it, coming away with about a tablespoon of salt in his palm. Meanwhile, someone else was wringing out his raincoat, and I had hidden myself behind the stroke-oar to avoid questions about the rivulet of blood that had seeped through my shirt from I-hadn't-figured-out-where-yet.

By some miracle, *all* of this went unnoticed by the head coach, and we were dismissed without further question.

We told the boys not to talk about what happened. So, naturally, the whole school found out by the next day.

Marty Zuehlke

American Marty Zuehlke of Austin Rowing Club in Texas is an artist, cartoonist, poet, writer, and masters rower and coach. Marty is also a very persuasive guy, as he recently discovered.

A Little Tick in Her Stroke

Not long ago I was coaching a young woman who was just picking up the sport, had tons of potential, and was doing pretty well. I asked her if she would trust me and do exactly what I said, and I would trust her to do it. She agreed.

I said to her, "You know, it would help your stroke to row with your feet out for a bit. You get a nice feel for the release and for the recovery that way."

About three months later, when she had progressed and was sprinting really well, I noticed that she had a little tick in her stroke. I thought maybe she had gotten a little bit of a cramp or something. I pulled up in my launch, looked in the boat and said, "Your feet are out!"

She said, "Well, you've never said to put them back in."

Sue and Bryan Storey

Dudley Storey OBE, one of the great icons of New Zealand rowing, recently passed away at the age of 77. Gold medallist in the men's coxed-fours at the 1968 Olympics in Mexico City, silver medallist in the men's coxless-fours at the 1972 Olympics in Munich, team manager under Harry Mahon at the 1984 Olympics in Los Angeles, Dudley was a friend and mentor to generations of Kiwi rowers and will be a role model forever.

In 2000, Sue and Bryan Storey and their three children, John, Richard and Jenny, emigrated from Cambridge in England to Christchurch, South Island of New Zealand. They had never heard of Dudley.

Regrettably, They Never Met

Although we were all very sporty in England – Bryan rugby and Sue hockey – rowing was one sport our family did not participate in during twenty years of living in Cambridge. All three children loved a variety of sport and showed good aptitude and early enthusiasm to "give anything a go", so whilst at prep school at St. Faiths Cambridge in England, they participated in and were members of first teams in the major school sports.

When we arrived in Christchurch, our two boys were enrolled at St. Andrews College, where John and later Richard were introduced to the sport of rowing. When she turned 11, Jenny moved to an all-girls school, Rangi Ruru.

John was a strong young man, and with encouraging coaches, he enjoyed the routine and discipline that rowing demanded. He started competing at 15 in his age group, mainly in small boats as St. Andrews at that time did not have enough rowers to produce consistently good eights.

John only ever won a bronze medal at the Maadi Cup Regatta[21]. However, he did set a NZ record on the erg as a lightweight which still stands to this day.

His younger brother, Richard, went on to win two Maadi Cup golds in double sculls, and two bronzes in quad sculls in different age groups.

Over the years at Maadi Cup, the infrastructure improved, including TV coverage and even commentary on the side of the bank that you could hear and understand!!! Each time our children competed as regular members of top school crews, the commentator would mention them by name and invariably link them to Dudley Storey, a stalwart of NZ rowing unknown to us and definitely not a relative. Over the years, these comments became more regular, linking our now proficient rowers with the Dudley Storey name. Time to put things right, and over several seasons the commentators were eventually convinced that we were not related.

Jenny had spent several years as a spectator watching her brothers row, so when her time came she grasped it with both hands.

By the end of her Rangi Ruru career, she had won the most medals of anyone in the history of the school, winning the Dawn Cup (under-18 fours) two times and Levin Jubilee Cup (under-18 eights) three times, twice in stroke-seat. At 16 she was selected for the South Island under-18 team. In 2009, at the age of 17 she was selected for NZ juniors leading up to the World Championships, held in Brive-la-Gaillarde, France, stroking the eight to silver behind a strong USA team.

---

[21] annual New Zealand Secondary Schools Championship

She got her revenge the following year, being part of the gold-winning junior four, racing at Račice, Czech Republic.

She now plays for the "Blacksticks" – NZ national hockey team – with over forty caps, while studying physiotherapy following on from a science degree. Her sights are set on Tokyo and making the NZ Olympic hockey squad.

After St. Andrews, Richard was unable to continue rowing as he pursued medical studies in Dunedin, but John joined Avon Rowing Club and the Southern High Performance Centre in Christchurch whilst studying for a four-year Mechanical Engineering degree at Canterbury University.

At 22 at the Nationals Regatta, rowing with Hamish Bond stroking, the Southern RPC won the fours and eights, John being awarded his first "Red Coat", emblematic of a Premier NZ National title. He was then selected for the 2009 NZ under-23 team, winning world gold in the men's coxed-fours in Račice.

Following that, John was selected for the NZ Elite team, and he has been a member of the Kiwi squad ever since, apart from taking a year out in 2013 to finish his Engineering degree.

In 2016, John was selected for the NZ quad which just missed qualifying for the Olympics in Rio, but he had beaten Mahe Drysdale in the single sculls event at the Cambridge Cup Regatta, setting the course record on Lake Karapiro, and so he became the sculling reserve for Rio.

He raced in the men's single sculls at the World Cup Regatta just before Rio, making the A final alongside Mahe, a history-making moment for New Zealand Rowing, having two single scullers making the same A final.

Just four weeks before Rio, the NZ quad was added to the Olympic field after the Russians were banned for using performance enhancing drugs. John was quickly flown back to NZ to reunite with the rest of his crew – all had been on holiday and not rowed since their last chance to qualify early in the summer – and they had the impossible task of trying to regain their competitive speed in four weeks' time.

Needless to say, it was a tough campaign but a great experience. John felt they could have done so much better with a proper lead up to the Games. [They placed tenth of ten. George Bridgewater, also appearing in this book, rowed 3-seat, just ahead of John in 2.]

Still, having a point to prove, John was selected for the Kiwi men's double in 2017 with Chris Harris. They won gold at the two World Cups they attended, Poznan and Lucerne, and in between competed and won the Double Sculls Challenge Cup at Henley, to the delight of our English relatives who came to support him. He received the cup with his partner while proudly wearing his Cambridge (UK) St. Faiths prep school leavers tie. They will enter the 2017 World Championships in Sarasota, Florida undefeated, and time will tell if another success is on the cards for the Storey family.

We do hope John and his siblings have done their part to carry on the proud Storey name within the NZ rowing community and that Dudley can be pleased.

To this day, John is often asked if he is related to the great man. Regrettably, they never met.

[At the 2017 World Championships, John Storey and his partner Chris Harris capped an undefeated season by winning the World Championship in the men's double sculls. The Storey saga continues.]

Dudley Storey

And now it seems appropriate for us to hear from Dudley himself.

I became very good friends with Dudley Storey in 2010 at the World Championships on Lake Karapiro. In 2012, my wife Susan and I sat with Dudley and his wife Paula at the 2012 Olympics at Eton-Dorney, a treasured memory for us now that he is gone.

Dudley was an inveterate story teller, and whenever he talked about rowing, his eyes would flash, the words tumbling out in his thick Kiwi accent, a raw physicality to his frame and enormous vitality in the way he moved. His smile would fill the room.

I present below his story of the 1968 Mexico City Olympics in his own words.

First some background.

At only 5'10", Dudley Storey was an improbable candidate for an Olympic Gold Medal in rowing. He had started his competitive career at Sacred Heart College in Auckland in 1954 at the age of 14, and won his first Red Coat four years later. He rowed at the 1964 Olympics in the Kiwi coxed-four and at the 1966 World Championships in the sixth-place NZ eight.

By Mexico City, he had been rowing half his life.

Prior to the regatta, all the talk was about the 7,316-foot altitude and its impact on athletes. Racing there would be a journey into the unknown for all crews competing.

The Kiwi Blitz

We were getting information, particularly from the medical people, that we would be lucky if somebody didn't *die* in Mexico. "It's high altitude, and you better take spares," and all that stuff, and so the basic premise at the time was that the Four were the spares for the Eight. We were going to do the fill-in job if something actually transpired, which of course it didn't. It was all a bit of a washover in the end.

But because the Four was what they used to call a 'B' crew in those days in New Zealand, they put us in the position of *not* actually knowing until maybe about eight weeks prior to the Olympics as to whether or not we were going to even *go*, so we did a twelve-week training in Christchurch still fully unaware whether or not we were going.

I can describe the row to you when we first knew we were fast. It was only about two weeks prior to the announcement by our national Olympic organization as to who was going to go and who wasn't, and I think it was a still pretty close run thing, to be honest.

We were training at the Avon Rowing Club[22], and that day we were scheduled to go across what we called the Sumner Estuary. We rowed down the Avon River as far the last bridge [about 4k], and then it was about a 5 or 6k run across to the far side of the estuary.

And we were *very* keen to run ourselves against the Eight this particular day. God only knows why, but we said, "*We* are going to get to the far side *first!*" and we worked out a little strategy as to how we were going to do it.

First thing you have to do, of course, is get through that last little bridge on the river in first place because only one boat at a time could get through, so we managed to achieve that, and we started off across the estuary probably about two lengths in front of them.

We managed to gather their speed, rating about two or three points higher obviously. And then we said, "We are not going to let these bastards pass... today we are *not* going to let them pass."

---

[22] the same place John Storey would train at half a century later.

Bob Page was steering the Eight, and we overheard him say, "Come on. We've got to get alongside this four. They are just sitting on your bow." So they went up one point.

They were doing about 18. We were doing 21 or so. As soon as they started to creep up, we inched it up a couple. After the first k had gone past, the second k comes up.

"They're still sitting on your bow, so get past," and up they went another notch.

Well, by the time we got to the far side of the estuary, they were at 34 or something, and we were at about 38, and we had nowhere else to go, not by the end of that 6k, and they got us *right* at the very, very end... but we said to ourselves, "We now *know* that this is fast. *We now know!*" Because they just couldn't get past, no matter what they did, and that was a *very* fast eight! They were set for a medal!

Anyway, we got to go to Mexico, and we sort of decided what to do about racing at altitude when we got there. We'd heard all these stories, and we were watching the reactions of other people, the Germans, Americans, Brits and the Aussies, anybody, and they were all talking about this "even splits down the race course" stuff.

For argument's sake, if you thought the race was going to be done in 6 minutes, you did 1:30, 1:30, 1:30, 1:30. That gives you 6 minutes.

Well, we sort of thought, "*Stuff that!* If *that's* the way everybody else is going to race, we are going to have to find another strategy. We've *got* to find some other way."

I remember riding in the bus coming back from the course one day, sharing a seat with this American. I didn't know him and he didn't know me from a bar of soap, but he says to me, rather brashly I thought at the time, "I'm here to win m'self a Gold Medal."

And so he told me his whole life story. Americans being Americans, it's what you *do!*

One of the questions I asked him was, "How long have you been rowing?" and he said, "Four years."

All I said in return was, "Four years? Hmm," because I wasn't giving any information back at all. Not that I was being coy, but I wasn't asked for any so I didn't offer any.

But I'd been around *fourteen* years by that time.

At the end of it, I asked him what event he was in.

"Oh, I'm in the four-with." And I thought, "Well there ain't no way this prick's beating *me*, not with *that* load of stuff!"

But, you know it was honest, and it was self-belief on his part... and he was a big guy as well.

I relayed the story to our guys, about this bloke goin' on about how good they were.

After that, they never had a *chance.*

Coming back to our race strategy, we started practising going out between 600 and 700 metres and then burying the boat and trying to break away from the other boats.

And we did it in the heat. I think we actually took eight seconds out of the field, including the Americans, inside 25 strokes.

1 NZL	7:12.19
2 ROM	7:16.56
3 USA	7:21.39
4 CUB	7:41.11

We thought to ourselves, *"This works!"*

The problem was when we got to the end, we were so *shagged* we couldn't get out of the *boat...* but nobody knew that [big laugh] because the other little strategy that we had was that *regardless* of what happens, when we hear the bell go at the end, we've just *got* to keep on rowing to the dock.

We're not going to stop. Just... *don't... stop!* Another 200 metres, all we have to do is just keep rowing. Don't do anything!

Well, we sat there for 20 minutes... unable to get out... but by that time we had recovered, and we thought, "This *works!* We just have to refine it."

And that's *all* we did!

Originally in the heat it was 20 strokes, and we got about 25 out of it. We got an extra 5 for nothing.

"Oh, this is pretty good!"

The next time, in the semi-final, we did 25 strokes, and we got *30* out of it.

1 NZL	6:48.65
2 USA	6:54.22
3 ITA	6:58.24
4 ARG	7:02.25
5 FRG	7:06.45
6 NED	7:08.68

So in the final we did *30* strokes, and the 30 was just enough. That was the tipping point. By the time of the final, an American magazine was calling it 'the Kiwi blitz.'

And that's how we raced the final. We didn't want to get sucked into what the medicos were saying. We *know* we're fast, and all we have to do is bury these people somewhere down the course!

[Dudley ended his story to me right there. I suppose he figured he didn't have to blow his own trumpet any further, that the rest was history anyway, and I could look it up for myself, which of course I did.

In the Olympic final, the Kiwis pulled 3.11 seconds ahead of the East German boat at the 1,000, with the rest of the field a half-length or more further astern. That was it. They expanded their lead to nearly five seconds at the 1,500 and still had 2.58 seconds in hand as they crossed the line.It was New Zealand's first-ever Olympic rowing medal.]

1 NZL	6:45.62
2 GDR	6:48.20
3 SUI	6:49.04
4 ITA	6:49.54
5 USA	6:51.41
6 URS	7:00.00

Göran Buckhorn

Rowing has a long and rich history, as the author of this tale discovered growing up. A Swede now living in Connecticut, USA, Göran Buckhorn is a magazine editor and freelance culture scribe, member of the British Association of Rowing Journalists, a Director of the Friends of Rowing History, and founder and editor of the rowing history website *Hear the Boat Sing*, Rowing Blog of the Year in 2012.

Göran is still a member of Malmö RK.

My First Outing – And In An 'Olympic Boat', Sort Of…

For more than a century, rowing had taken place in my hometown of Malmö in the south of Sweden, on the canals, along the shoreline and out on the Öresund strait between Sweden and Denmark. I discovered rowing in my early teens when two of my childhood friends, Per Ekström and Ola Nilsson, dragged me down to the venerable Malmö Roddklubb to let me have a try. On a sunny, warm day in May 1973, I found myself sitting in a boat for my inaugural row.

It was an old, wooden clinker-built inrigger coxed-four. Inriggers – a wide boat where the oarlocks are mounted on the gunwales and the rowers sit on sliding seats in a zigzag way – are still used in the Nordic countries today on rough waters along the coastline and on rivers and lakes.

In 1912, the inrigger coxed-fours event unexpectedly was included as a boat class in the Stockholm Olympics. Prominent rowing nations protested its inclusion, saying that a boat type of this kind had no business in the Olympics, and after 1912, the inrigger would never return to the Olympic Games.

Three members of Malmö RK rowed in the 1912 Swedish Olympic inrigger coxed-four. How did they do at the Olympics 61 years before I pulled an oar for the first time? They reached the final and won the Silver Medal behind Denmark. It would take Sweden another 44 years before the country took its second Olympic medal in rowing, a Silver in the coxed-four-oared *shells* at Ballarat, Australia, in 1956.

Needless to say, while rowing in that inrigger in May 1973, I was totally oblivious to the boat type's short Olympic history and to Malmö RK's past Olympic glory. I was hard at work trying to coordinate my oar and the rolling seat I was sitting on.

The cox was an older fellow – or so he seemed to be in my eyes – whose colourful language was of another world. Never before or after, have I heard such language coming from the cox seat; come to think about it, not ever outside a boat either.

What I did not know at the time was that the cox, Mr. Larsson, had 21 years earlier been in the Malmö RK crew who tried to get selected for the 1952 Olympic Games. Although, they failed to be nominated to race in Helsinki, they were chosen as Olympic torchbearers. The Malmö eight was one of 1,416 torchbearers who carried the Olympic flame from Olympia in Greece to Helsinki in Finland. On 1 July 1952, the M.S. *Marstrandsfjorden* took the torch across the Öresund strait from Copenhagen to Malmö's outer harbour, where the ship was met by the Malmö RK's eight. The crew then rowed the torch into the canals that surround the Old Town.

Being a part of the Olympic Torch Relay for the 1952 Olympic Games was a great honour for Malmö RK, and it was with great pride that members of the crew told us youngsters the story two decades later.

On that first outing on the canals around the Old Town of Malmö, we rowed through two beautiful parks and under nearly 20 bridges. It gave me a totally different perspective on Malmö, and well before we returned to the boathouse, I was infatuated by my new sport.

Although I never became a star, I am grateful for everything rowing has given me through the years. Ever since that day in May 1973, I have continued to look backwards in life – for the two last decades as a rowing historian.

Volker Nolte

One of the most memorable characters in the long history of world rowing is German-born Volker Nolte, recently retired professor of biomechanics at the University of Western Ontario, Canada. Prolific author, champion coach and mentor to a generation of rowing scientists, here he describes one of his many historic accomplishments.

Kolbe's Last Chance

The rowing story that comes to my mind right away, because it was very special to me, was developing the sliding rigger single. I did not invent the sliding rigger. It was patented 100 years earlier, and it was tried several times over this 100 years. Literally, every ten years, someone tried to use it.

I think I was the first one who realized how the principle worked and that it for sure would be an advantage to use it. This happened during my studies for PhD when I developed a computer program where I could simulate certain situations. For example, if someone has longer legs or a heavier bodyweight, lighter bodyweight, and so on, and I also could change certain parameters on the boat, so I changed it to the sliding rigger. It became immediately clear from a theoretical point of view that it MUST be faster.

So, I went to my friend, Leo Wolloner, who was the foreman at Empacher Company – the boat builder in Germany. I told him about it, and he was not very keen of it. At first, he said, "Okay, this has been done already – 100 times. No one believes in it, blah, blah." So, it took me about half a year to convince him, but he finally built a prototype boat.[23]

It turned out, actually, that this would be the prototype of the wing rigger. He built one out of carbon fibre because his specialty was using composite materials. He was one of the first ones who did this in a very special way.

So, he built this boat, and of course, when you build a prototype, you do not know all the tricks that are involved. For example, the seat. He put in a normal seat fixed to the boat. I tested it and discovered that if you push off the foot stretcher, you will fall off the seat, so you have to build a seat that has a lip at the end that holds your butt so you cannot slide off. But then, of course, the seat has to be really formed to your butt because, if you do not do this, you get very quickly blisters. I went all through this – falling off the seat, getting blisters on my butt, and so on – and this was only one thing.

Then, of course, it needed to be constructed so that you could actually use a full slide and such things, so it took me some time to do this.

When it was ready, the top people didn't want to use it. Literally, no one wanted to use it. It was left to me to row the boat. I had already retired, so I started to get a little bit back in shape. But then I had to row in official races and did way better than I should have with my abilities. For example, I came third at the German Championship against Peter-Michael Kolbe and such top people. I was beating national team athletes. I used it in a 10-kilometre race for the national team, and I won in a

---

[23] The boat is now on display in the Rowing Gallery of the River & Rowing Museum in Henley-on-Thames, England.

record time and such things, and then people started to recognize it, but still no one wanted to row it.

It only happened when Peter-Michael Kolbe had lost for a whole year against another West German rower, Georg Agrikola. Kolbe's last chance was to use the sliding rigger, and he did it at the Lucerne Regatta. Empacher built a boat for him because, I mean, he's taller than I and he needed a little bit better boat.

He used the boat in the race, and not only did he beat the West German guys, so he won the internal qualification for the World Championships, but he also faced Uwe Mundt, the very big talent from the East German group. The East Germans were bragging, "Oh, this will not work. Mundt will beat him easily," and so on. In fact, Kolbe won, and this was psychologically devastating for Mundt. He never rowed a single again after that.

Then Kolbe rowed the boat at the world championship and won easily. This was 1981. In 1982, a sliding rigger boat was used by the first six. Then, in 1983, the boat was used by eleven out of the twelve A and B semifinalists.

But then political opposition was building. The East Germans obviously hated it because a West German had beat the East Germans with better technology and such things, and they couldn't leave this as is. So, they started to lobby against it. And then the other one, this was very interesting. Pertti Karppinen could not use a sliding rigger boat. He didn't feel comfortable, so he actually went out of the single and into the double with his brother, but they never made it to world champion. They made silver medal but never world champion. The Scandinavian countries started building a lobby, too.

It became political, and there were all kinds of dumb arguments that the boat would be too expensive and all this stuff. I tried to counter this. I gave a presentation at the FISA Coaches Conference, clarifying that the extra cost was minimal relative to the overall cost. Plus, after a while, you would actually see benefits from it, and one benefit was, of course, the wing rigger.

In the end, it was Kolbe who really rowed this boat very well, rowed it perfectly. He won the world championship in the boat in '81 and '83, but the lobbying by the Eastern Bloc and the Scandinavians was stronger, so FISA prohibited the boat starting in 1984. Of course, after it was forbidden, Kolbe came second at the '84 Olympic Games against Karppinen, who was a faster guy.

The interesting thing, again, and I said this at my presentation at the FISA Coaches Conference: if you prohibit technological development, you diminish our sport.

I also said that most likely in ten years everyone would row with wing rigger. Every boat builder actually built then a sliding rigger boat. The American boat builder, Van Dusen had one, Stämpfli had one, Hudson had one, the East Germans had one. All these boat building companies had their sliding riggers, but Van Dusen did the following thing: he had the foot stretchers attached underneath the wing and then, of course, the whole thing moving. When the sliding rigger was outlawed, he simply took the foot stretchers off the wing, put the foot stretchers in the boat, put the wing on top of the boat, and here we go. This was the prototype of the wing rigger.

Sure enough, nowadays everyone rows wing rigger because it's such an easy construction compared to the side boat riggers. You don't need shoulders anymore. It's much easier to build and so on.

George Bridgewater

George Bridgewater, from Wellington, New Zealand, won World Gold in 2005 and Olympic Silver in 2008 in the men's coxless-pairs. Below he muses on the continuing role of rowing in his life.

Contemplating Outcomes

Sport can be very black & white, at least in contrast to many other things in life where there is a lot of gray in between. Often we are encouraged early in life to get as much sport in as possible. Perhaps parents feel it teaches their kids things theory cannot and how to deal with situations or how to deal with people. But often this stops as the teenage years roll on and school finishes – organised sport is no longer as easy as stepping out of class and onto the field. Work takes up more time, and, if we're lucky, exercise to stay fit and healthy becomes something that is squeezed in between nights at the pub.

Not many people experience sport as an all-consuming roller coaster ride that most full-time athletes do. Functioning in a world that is so black & white, so immediate in its feedback every day, has been exhilarating for me. Can you imagine four years of work coming down to one six-minute performance, where you need to be physically, mentally, emotionally *en pointe* to measure your effort for the last four years? What if just one member of your team got injured or sick? For something that is so physical, the contrasting delicacy of the situation is so stark that it's almost comical. In training, you can win a session in the morning and feel confidence sky high, and then come back later that day and lose a session to the same opponent. Your body and mind sharpen to living in a competitive environment, and you begin to be ready for anything because that's what you are practicing for.

For me, after I left rowing competitively, I embraced the life of an office worker. Sitting in a chair for twelve hours a day on the 36th floor in Hong Kong, gym after work two weekdays plus Saturday mornings, weekends free to do what I wanted, bars, restaurants, holidays etc. The novelty lasted for a bit, it was great to be having a 'job' and getting an income.

But after a few months I realised I wasn't near to being world class at this new job, and it became disappointing to deal with the fact that 'you're not that good at what you do.' I don't think this was specific to the job or industry I was working in, just that when you try something new and worthwhile, you're most likely not to be all that good at it to begin with.

After a couple of years, I figured out how to get by, but I also realised how people change according to your standing in the hierarchy – which obviously changes significantly from organization to organization. The learning was ongoing every day, which was one of the big upsides, but after two years I had learnt enough to not say stupid things and which people were to be avoided. From that point on, as I came up for air and took a look around, my confidence grew... but satisfaction did not come with it. As a cog in a machine, any member of our team could take a day off or be on holiday, and the rest of the team functioned perfectly well. This didn't sit particularly well with me, and I sought something else, something more lucid.

It's my belief that, for many spectators, sport is craved on a primal level because of its physically- and emotionally-charged unpredictability. And it's very clear who is the best at the end of the day. Humans are outcome-oriented creatures; watch a movie and there is always a sense of closure at the end – and if there is not, we will usually lament the fact. Sport offers the ultimate non-fatal short timeframe outcome – and we like to believe it is played fairly and to the best of individual ability. With corruption or doping, sport becomes infected – outcomes become scripted and predictable, and sport will gradually become less and less attractive. Our international governing bodies and committees hold so much responsibility in keeping things on the right track, and in these times it's just so difficult to have faith across the board that sport and sport management is pure.

To me, one of the beautiful things about rowing is that money hasn't quite corrupted it (although the wolf is never far from the gates when the sport is brought into the Olympic fold). International rowers race maybe twice a year and those races are generally dead boring-to-watch – even ever-supportive parents usually only fly to the destinations that have the better holiday bolt-ons. It's not a spectator sport, so it is not a sport that generates a lot of money. Like many things, the presence of money determines the size, shape and direction of the sphere. And with higher cash stakes involved, the more likely it is that doping lurks beneath the surface.

The people involved in rowing generally aren't naturally gifted athletes, often large people with limited coordination, which has ruled them out from other more popular sports. They don't play for money. They play to challenge what is possible from minds and bodies that otherwise would have gone out and gotten an office job somewhere. They've put starting a career or a family substantially on hold to follow a passion in which ability peaks only too early in life. What else could you be the best in the world at by age 25?

It's been a hell of a journey returning to rowing after five years away – and after the first step of making the decision to return, not a day has been daunting.

So despite my failing to qualify for the Olympic Games in Rio,[24] which will be held in a couple of months' time, there are no regrets about putting career on hold. The journey has been rewarding, and most days have been exciting, rather than arduous.

It's hard to explain a lot of what I have learned, particularly the minutiae, but understanding what makes me feel happy has been particularly useful. I've realised that I am a person who needs to understand what my role in the big picture is, and while this may sound obvious, in some settings it's not really apparent.

Learning can come from both positive and negative situations, enhancing the arsenal with which we complete tasks, but to be around passionate and courageous people who are clear in purpose is especially endearing and something I will continue to prioritise wherever it is a possibility.

---

[24] After writing this tale, Bridgewater actually did represent New Zealand in Rio, rowing with John Storey in the tenth-placed Kiwi Men's Quad.

Xeno Müller

Xeno Müller, U.S. Collegiate Varsity Eights Champion while at Brown University, won the 1996 Olympic Men's Singles Gold Medal for his native Switzerland. During his career he was coached by a number of the most respected rowing coaches in the World, including New Zealander Harry Mahon, Australian Marty Aitken and American Steve Gladstone.

He and his family now live in Southern California where he produces indoor rowing workout DVDs and runs *The Iron Oarsman*, an indoor rowing studio.

Rowing Changed the Course of My Life

Imagine seeing the sun ablaze in the sky and the mist rising from the water as you start your morning workout. Or, paddling back to the dock in the evening with the stars shining bright in the sky, your body tired, but your spirit raised with a sense of accomplishment. These are the moments all rowers share.

I have been very fortunate to have spent most of my life on or near the water. In my mind, there is nothing more peaceful than being on the water. As a teenager in France I was very fortunate to live near the Fontainebleau/Avon rowing club. Like most rowers I know, I was quickly hooked and became obsessed with learning more and getting faster.

It wasn't until much later in life that I realized how very lucky I actually was to start with great coaching and to continue to have the most successful coaches in the world train me throughout my rowing career.

Over the years, I have heard so many stories of kids just like me who had a very different experience, their coaches constantly yelling, 'PULL HARDER!' or, 'You're not mentally tough enough!' My coaches were demanding, but they were also part of a coaching family tree where the technical aspects of the rowing stroke were passed down, as well as the secrets of physical and mental training. This is why you can trace the vast majority of collegiate and Olympic Gold Medal crews back to a handful of influential and skilled elite coaches.

Young high school rowers, their families and spectators often think that you have to be the biggest and strongest to win gold in rowing. They look at me and say, 'You are huge! Of course you won!' The truth is, when you look at who I beat over all those years, most often I was neither the biggest nor the strongest. I was the FASTEST, and that was because rowing, like most sports, has a large skill component.

Like other Gold Medal Olympic athletes, I worked very hard to achieve my dreams, but I did not do it alone. It also took a very supportive family, wonderful coaches and great friends. Everyone has doubts, disappointments and bouts of depression. The death of my father was a very difficult time in my life. He never saw me cross the finish line to earn Gold at the 1996 Olympic Games. It was my support network who helped get me through those tough times, and they continue to support me today.

As I sit here in Costa Mesa, California, I feel blessed to have the good fortune to pass down the secrets of elite rowing to a new generation of rowers. The sport of rowing changed the course of my life.

Frans Göbel

The last word goes to Dutch sculler Frans Göbel, today a physician and loyal member of De Hoop in Amsterdam. In 1989 and 1990 he was the Men's World Lightweight Singles Champion for the Netherlands.

September

I have a friend, about 30 or 32. He started rowing when he was 27, and he enjoyed it very well. He did it every day and he loved it, and he was writing stories about it... and then he called me two weeks ago, and he said, "Last summer, I started dancing – you know, ballet. I didn't row for a few months, and now I have started rowing again, and I don't enjoy it anymore.

"Frans, why am I not enjoying it anymore? What do I have to do?"

He got me to thinking about why do *I* like rowing. I thought, "What is the reason?" because I'm now rowing for about 45 years... so a very long time.

Why do I still like to row? I'm not so fast anymore, I'm not so strong anymore, and so my friend's question forced me to ask myself the same question. "What makes rowing fun? What is rowing REALLY to me?"

For me, what's really special about rowing is that, even when I was a *very* good rower, when I was on the top level, you know, I sometimes had a training that didn't go well. And then, I had to adjust something. I had to think about it, or I had to relax. I had to get better. Most times, I could repair this failure in my rowing, I could repair it within a training or within a half-training.

Even now, sometimes I go out rowing... and it only hurts. I go out, and I hardly can go in my boat or I hardly can come out of the boat. I return and it's heavy and my muscles are sore... and then I am sitting, and I think, "I don't like this. Why I am doing this?"

Even now.

But then last weekend I was rowing, and it was quite nasty weather. It was raining hard and it was windy, but then suddenly I felt, "I'm now rowing for 46 years, and now THIS training TODAY, after 46 years, NOW, I understand what I have to do!"

That's so special in rowing because you think it's a simple movement, do you understand? I did it at a very high level, and I still sometimes find out, "Shit, if I had this known thirty years ago, I could have been an incredibly good rower. I would have gone very, VERY fast – much faster than I did."

But it still happens, you know. Maybe it goes badly for me one day, and I go slow and I fight it, but maybe the next Sunday or Monday I go again... and then, really, THIS IS IT! I HAVE IT!

People learn.

So I said to my friend who had lost his love for rowing, "What you have to do is you have to be patient about this."

It was September, and I don't know how it is for you, but in our climate September is the most lovely rowing season there is. In September you have days when sometimes it's a kind of foggy in the morning. There is no wind, the water is flat, there is no noise, and you put your boat in the water... and you are alone.

You go very early in the morning – that's what I like, when there are no other rowers.

I have to tell you about ice skating because, you know, in Holland, sometimes, you have the water frozen. If you go ice skating, and you are the first one on new ice and nobody has touched this ice and you go ice skating on that ice, that's the same feeling if you row in September when it is foggy. You feel the stillness. Sometimes, you can just look out over the fog, and you are the only one and there is no noise. You only hear and feel the water dribbling under the boat, and it's going SO easily. It feels as if you don't have to do ANYTHING to make the boat go fast.

If you have that feeling for one time in the whole year, it will be a very good year.

Yes, I told my friend to be patient. And I think he will get it back because there WILL be one morning he goes out, and he has this feeling... and then he will be captivated again.

I think it will work like that because, in my case, it's been like that for about 47 years. For so long I'm in a boat.

It's September. In so many ways.

Printed in Poland
by Amazon Fulfillment
Poland Sp. z o.o., Wrocław